New Directions for
Institutional Research

Robert K. Toutkoushian
EDITOR-IN-CHIEF

J. Fredericks Volkwein
ASSOCIATE EDITOR

D0743451

Analyzing Faculty Work and Rewards:
Using Boyer's Four Domains of Scholarship

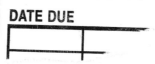

DATE DUE

John M. Braxton

EDITOR

Number 129 • Spring 2006
Jossey-Bass
San Francisco

ANALYZING FACULTY WORK AND REWARDS: USING BOYER'S FOUR DOMAINS OF SCHOLARSHIP
John M. Braxton (ed.)
New Directions for Institutional Research, no. 129
Robert K. Toutkoushian, Editor-in-Chief

NEW DIRECTIONS FOR INSTITUTIONAL RESEARCH (ISSN 0271-0579, electronic ISSN 1536-075X) is part of The Jossey-Bass Higher and Adult Education Series and is published quarterly by Wiley Subscription Services, Inc., A Wiley Company, at Jossey-Bass, 989 Market Street, San Francisco, California 94103-1741 (publication number USPS 098-830). Periodicals Postage Paid at San Francisco, California, and at additional mailing offices. POSTMASTER: Send address changes to New Directions for Institutional Research, Jossey-Bass, 989 Market Street, San Francisco, California 94103-1741.

SUBSCRIPTIONS cost $80.00 for individuals and $170.00 for institutions, agencies, and libraries. See order form at end of book.

EDITORIAL CORRESPONDENCE should be sent to Robert K. Toutkoushian, Educational Leadership and Policy Studies, Education 4220, 201 N. Rose Ave., Indiana University, Bloomington, IN 47405.

New Directions for Institutional Research is indexed in *College Student Personnel Abstracts, Contents Pages in Education,* and *Current Index to Journals in Education* (ERIC).

Microfilm copies of issues and chapters are available in 16mm and 35mm, as well as microfiche in 105mm, through University Microfilms Inc., 300 North Zeeb Road, Ann Arbor, Michigan 48106-1346.

www.josseybass.com

CONTENTS

EDITOR'S NOTES

In his influential book *Scholarship Reconsidered: Priorities of the Professoriate,* Boyer (1990) proposed that the definition of scholarship be broadened beyond the predominant emphasis on the scholarship of discovery to encompass the scholarship of integration, the scholarship of application, and the scholarship of teaching:

- Scholarship of discovery. This is traditional research and the scholarship of the creation or discovery of new knowledge. It requires creative and critical thought, research skills, publication in peer-reviewed journals and books, and presentations at disciplinary conferences.
- Scholarship of application. This involves the use of a scholar's disciplinary knowledge to address important individual, institutional, and societal problems. Those who engage in this type of work, also called *the scholarship of engagement and outreach,* must be able to solve problems of importance to diverse stakeholders (for example, policymakers, community members, and corporate leaders) and to communicate effectively with these audiences in language understandable to persons without disciplinary expertise.
- Scholarship of integration. This form of scholarship makes connections within and among disciplines. When disciplinary and interdisciplinary knowledge is synthesized, interpreted, and connected, the work brings new insight to original research (Braxton, Luckey, and Helland, 2002). The products include policy papers, reflective essays, research translations, popular press publications, synthesis of the literature on a topic, and textbooks.
- Scholarship of teaching. The scholarship of teaching is the development and improvement of pedagogical practices (Braxton, Luckey, and Helland, 2002). Effective teachers engage in scholarly teaching if they undertake assessment and evaluation to promote improvement in their own teaching practice. Scholarly teaching activity becomes scholarship of teaching when faculty members make their teaching public by opening it to review and critique by peers in their disciplines through publications and presentations.

Individual scholars engage in each of these scholarships as their professional roles, career stages, and research goals change over time. Understanding both the unique characteristics of the four domains and how work in one domain connects with and influences work in another provides faculty with a map of the broad territory of scholarly activity and recognizes the legitimacy of each different intellectual contribution.

NEW DIRECTIONS FOR INSTITUTIONAL RESEARCH, no. 129, Spring 2006   © Wiley Periodicals, Inc.
Published online in Wiley InterScience (www.interscience.wiley.com) • DOI: 10.1002/ir.167

Boyer's formulations sparked considerable scholarly attention primarily focused on clarifying the meaning of the domains of scholarship and on criteria and forms of documentation needed to assess scholarship across the four domains (Glassick, Huber, and Maeroff, 1997). This spate of literature and scholarly discussion coupled with a lapse of over fifteen years since the advancement of Boyer's perspective strongly indicates a need for a stock-taking of this literature.

In their book *Institutionalizing a Broader View of Scholarship Through Boyer's Four Domains* (2002), Braxton, Luckey, and Helland engaged in such a stocktaking. They empirically addressed the extent to which the four domains of scholarship have become institutionalized into the academic work of college and university faculty members. They also sought an understanding of the limitations and possibilities of institutionalization by focusing on factors that foster or impede the institutionalization of Boyer's formulations. These factors included state-level instruments of economic development, the academic reward structure, and graduate education.

O'Meara and Rice's edited volume, *Faculty Priorities Reconsidered* (2005), adds to this stocktaking by presenting case studies of efforts by colleges and universities to redefine faculty roles and rewards congruent with Boyer's perspective on broadening the definitional parameters of scholarship. It also assesses the impact of reform.

Despite the efforts of such stocktaking, some issues received little or no attention or require further consideration. This *New Directions for Institutional Research* volume delves further into Boyer's perspective on scholarship by addressing the putative interdependency of the four domains of scholarship, further consideration of altering the academic reward structure, the influence of state-level policies on the institutionalization of Boyer's perspective on scholarship, rethinking graduate education, and further reflections on the meaning of the scholarship of teaching.

The power of Boyer's efforts to broaden the boundaries of scholarship lies in the differentiation among four domains of scholarship: application, discovery, integration, and teaching. Such a differentiation points to the value of forms of scholarship other than discovery, the predominant form of scholarship currently valued and rewarded in higher educational institutions. This differentiation also creates the view that these four domains are mutually exclusive of one another.

Boyer (1990), however, acknowledged that these four domains "dynamically interact, forming an interdependent whole" (p. 25). Rice (1992) also recognizes their interdependency and posits that they form a conceptual whole that is as important as the sum of its parts. Moreover, Paulsen and Feldman (1995) assert that the four domains of scholarship comprise interdependent parts of a social action system focused on scholarship. In Chapter One, Carol L. Colbeck and Patty Wharton Michael present a case for the integration of the four domains of scholarship through the pursuit of public scholarship. They describe faculty engagement in public scholarship at The Pennsylvania State University and present a set of essential conditions for public scholarship and some implications of public scholarship for institutional research.

"Conceptual quagmire" best depicts the literature that debates the meaning of the scholarship of teaching (Braxton, Luckey, and Helland, 2002, p. 106). Braxton, Luckey and Helland attempt to clarify the objectives of the scholarship of teaching by positing that the "goal of the scholarship of teaching should be the development and improvement of pedagogical practice" (p. 106). In Chapter Two, Michael B. Paulsen and Kenneth A. Feldman bring further clarity to the meaning of the scholarship of teaching by conceptualizing it as a system of human action. In doing so, they extend Talcott Parsons's four function paradigm (Parsons and Platt, 1973; Parsons and Smelser, 1956) to classify dimensions of the scholarship of teaching and learning into each of the four functional imperatives of Parson's analytical framework: adaptation, goal attainment, pattern maintenance, and integration. To the function of pattern maintenance, they assign the scholarship of pedagogical content knowledge, which resonates well with Braxton, Luckey, and Helland's perspective on the goals of the scholarship of teaching. Paulsen and Feldman also allocate scholarly teaching to goal attainment, scholarly preparation of college teachings to adaptation, and scholarly evaluation and development of college teachers to the function of integration. The categorization of these aspects of college teaching that are often confused with the scholarship of teaching brings further clarity to the meaning of the scholarship of teaching. Professional activities for each of these functional imperatives are also delineated. Moreover, Paulsen and Feldman describe implications of the scholarship of teaching and learning as a human action system for institutional research and policy.

Although further institutionalization of the scholarship of teaching depends on a clear understanding of its objectives, attitudinal and structural factors present challenges. In Chapter Three, Kathleen McKinney uses a sociological lens to outline such attitudinal and structural factors. McKinney posits that the application of the outcomes of the scholarship of teaching and learning to the practice of day-to-day college teaching offers an approach to overcoming the limiting nature of such factors.

She discusses the ways in which such applications may occur at the level of the course, the level of the department and program, and the level of the institution.

Incorporation constitutes the most advanced form of institutionalization. It occurs when institutional values and norms associated with the object of institutionalization are embedded in the culture of the organization (Curry, 1991). Although the scholarship of discovery has attained the incorporation level of institutionalization, the scholarships of application, integration, and teaching have not (Braxton, Luckey, and Helland, 2002). Braxton, Luckey, and Helland point to the academic reward system and graduate education as impediments to the attainment of incorporation-level institutionalization of these domains of scholarship. Chapter Four concentrates on the role of graduate education in preparing future faculty members for engagement in not only the domain of discovery but also the scholarships of application, integration, and teaching. In this chapter, Ann E. Austin and Melissa McDaniels delineate a set of five competencies acquired through graduate education that support scholarship in the four domains. They also advance strategies to prepare students for engagement in the four domains of scholarship.

Chapters Five and Six focus on the academic reward system. In *Scholarship Reconsidered,* Boyer (1990) prescribed for various types of colleges and universities the domain or domains of scholarship appropriate to their institutional missions. In Chapter Five, John M. Braxton, William Luckey, and Patricia Helland assert that incorporation-level institutionalization of the scholarships of application, integration, and teaching depends on the value patterns toward these domains of scholarship that underlie the academic reward structures of comprehensive colleges and universities and liberal arts colleges. They use data collected from 882 faculty members in these types of colleges and universities to compare their formulations regarding these ideal value patterns toward the three domains of scholarship with the actual value patterns espoused at the level of college or university, academic department, and individual faculty members. Provocative conclusions about the potential for incorporation-level institutionalization emerge from the findings. Implications for policy and practice as well as recommendations for further research are presented.

In Chapter Six, KerryAnn O'Meara also concentrates on the academic reward system. She reports the findings of research conducted using the responses of 729 chief academic officers to identify both catalysts and barriers to the reform of institutional faculty reward systems. O'Meara also asked chief academic officers to assess how much support they perceive faculty at their college or university give to the broadening of the definition of scholarship that Boyer advocated. She presents some implications for understanding the impact of Boyer's perspective on scholarship as well as implications for research with particular attention to topics for study by institutional research officers.

Although Braxton, Luckey, and Helland (2002) describe the role of state policies and practices regarding economic development in fostering the institutionalization of the scholarship of application, scholars ignore the role that state accountability policies play in influencing faculty members to engage in the domains of scholarship described by Boyer. William R. Doyle offers a framework for addressing this issue in Chapter Seven. He applies strategic response theory to develop hypotheses about the type of response public colleges and universities will exhibit as a consequence of state policies to encourage the scholarship of teaching, discovery, and application.

Institutional research officers will find this volume useful to the practice of institutional research. Boyer's perspective presents many challenges to colleges and universities wishing to adopt some or all of his formulations, and the chapter authors offer insights into these challenges. Institutional research officers shoulder a large share of the responsibility for the institutionalization of Boyer's perspective at individual colleges and universities. To assist them in such efforts, most chapters offer suggestions for the role of institutional research. Scholars of higher education interested in faculty professional role performance, chief academic affairs officers, and college and university presidents will also find this volume useful to their practice.

Although some nettlesome issues remain, this volume confronts some of the pressing issues regarding the institutionalization of Boyer's perspective on scholarship.

John M. Braxton
Editor

References

Boyer, E. L. *Scholarship Reconsidered: Priorities of the Professoriate.* Princeton, N.J.: Carnegie Foundation for the Advancement of Teaching, 1990.

Braxton, J. M., Luckey, W., and Helland, P. *Institutionalizing a Broader View of Scholarship Through Boyer's Four Domains.* ASHE-ERIC Higher Education Report, vol. 29, no. 2. San Francisco: Jossey-Bass, 2002.

Curry, B. K. "Institutionalization: The Final Phase of the Organizational Change Process." *Administrator's Notebook,* 1991, 35(1), 1–5.

Glassick, C. E., Huber, M. T., and Maeroff, G. I. *Scholarship Assessed: Evaluation of the Professoriate.* San Francisco: Jossey-Bass, 1997.

O'Meara, K., and Rice, R. E. (eds.). *Faculty Priorities Reconsidered: Rewarding Multiple Forms of Scholarship.* San Francisco: Jossey-Bass, 2005.

Parsons, T., and Platt, G. M. *The American University.* Cambridge, Mass.: Harvard University Press, 1973.

Parsons, T., and Smelser, N. J. *Economy and Society.* New York: Free Press, 1956.

Paulsen, M. B., and K. A. Feldman. "Toward a Reconceptualization of Scholarship: A Human Action System with Functional Imperatives." *Journal of Higher Education,* 1995, 66(6), 615–640.

Rice, R. E. "Toward a Broader Conception of Scholarship: The American Context." In T. G. Whiston and R. L. Geiger (eds.), *Research and Higher Education: The United Kingdom and the United States.* Buckingham, England: Society for Research into Higher Education and the Open University, 1992.

JOHN M. BRAXTON is professor of education in the Higher Education Leadership and Policy Program of the Department of Leadership, Policy and Organizations, Peabody College of Vanderbilt University.

1

The authors argue for integrating Boyer's four domains through the pursuit of public scholarship.

The Public Scholarship: Reintegrating Boyer's Four Domains

Carol L. Colbeck, Patty Wharton Michael

The case that all dimensions of academic work, not just research, should be valued has been well advanced by the articulation of multiple domains of scholarship, specification of how to evaluate them, and investigation of the extent to which faculty engage in them and administrators evaluate them. There may be hidden hazards to articulating and evaluating the domains of academic work separately, however. The more that academic work is conceived as separate tasks, the less likely it is that faculty may be able to accomplish their professional work as an integrated whole (Colbeck, 2002). In this chapter, we argue for public scholarship as a professional model of academic work that resynthesizes the scholarly domains, while valuing their interdependent contributions to the whole. Public scholarship is

> scholarly activity generating new knowledge through academic reflection on issues of community engagement. It integrates research, teaching, and service. It does not assume that useful knowledge simply flows outward from the university to the larger community. It recognizes that new knowledge is created in its application in the field, and therefore benefits the teaching and research mission of the university [Yapa, 2006, p. 73].

Because public scholarship integrates all domains of faculty work, it must meet the criteria for scholarship articulated by Hutchings and Schulman (1999): it involves systematic inquiry and results in publicly

NEW DIRECTIONS FOR INSTITUTIONAL RESEARCH, no. 129, Spring 2006 © Wiley Periodicals, Inc.
Published online in Wiley InterScience (www.interscience.wiley.com) • DOI: 10.1002/ir.168

observable community property that is open to critique and available for others to use and develop. The concept and practice of public scholarship evolved from the land grant university mission of developing, disseminating, and applying knowledge as part of enlightened and effective participation in democracy (Cohen, 2001) and recent reconceptualizations of faculty work (Boyer, 1990; Kellogg Commission on the Future of State and Land-Grant Universities, 2000).

Labeling and Evaluating Different Domains of Academic Work

Concerned that the core teaching, research, and service purposes of academic work are increasingly fragmented and unbalanced, authors of two national reports renamed these purposes in an effort to reframe faculty work. Ernest Boyer, then president of the Carnegie Foundation for the Advancement of Teaching, proposed in 1990 that faculty work should be understood in terms of "four separate, yet overlapping functions" (p. 16): the scholarships of discovery, integration, application, and teaching. Similarly, the authors of the Kellogg Commission *Reports on the Future of State and Land-Grant Universities* argued in their sixth report (2000) that such institutions describe their responsibilities as learning, discovery, and engagement to renew their covenant with the public.

When the four domains of scholarship were articulated in *Scholarship Reconsidered* (Boyer, 1990), many higher education administrators and faculty were pleased with the well-reasoned argument that several dimensions of faculty work should be evaluated, and therefore valued, as much as research or discovery. Boyer asserted that "the full range of faculty talent must be more creatively assessed" (p. 34) because the scholarships of integration (interpreting and making interdisciplinary connections), application (engaging in the solution of socially consequential problems), and teaching (transmitting, transforming, and extending knowledge) might remain undervalued if ways to evaluate them fairly remained ambiguous.

Glassick, Huber, and Maeroff addressed the problem of how to bring clarity and some degree of uniformity to the evaluation of all four domains of scholarship in *Scholarship Assessed* (1997). Their criteria for evaluating the scholarships of integration, application, and teaching mirrored long-accepted criteria for evaluating the scholarship of discovery, commonly known as research. They asserted that work in each domain is scholarly to the extent that the scholar has (1) stated important and achievable goals, (2) demonstrated adequate knowledge of relevant literature and skills, (3) applied appropriate methods effectively, (4) achieved goals that add to knowledge in the field, (5) presented results clearly and with integrity, and (6) critically reflected on the value of the work. Although communicating the results of scholarships of discovery, application, integration, and teaching need not be restricted to refereed publications, Glassick, Huber, and Maeroff insisted that scholarly work must be documented to allow for peer review.

Various ways of documenting discovery, application, integration, and teaching were explored by Braxton, Luckey, and Helland (2002). They investigated the extent to which each of the four forms of scholarship has become institutionalized using documentation of faculty activities, unpublished scholarly outcomes, and publications as evidence. Their 1999 survey of nearly fifteen hundred faculty at five types of institutions showed that despite efforts to value all domains of academic work, the scholarship of discovery is still perceived as the most legitimate and important domain.

Consequences of Differential Evaluation of Work Domains

An unintended consequence of teasing apart the various domains of faculty scholarship may be reinforcement of a trend to divide the synergistic complexity of faculty work into distinct and ever more separable components. Boyer acknowledged that there might be some danger in dividing "intellectual functions that are inseparably tied together" (p. 25). Separating discovery, application, integration, and teaching into distinct categories for evaluation may do as much to fragment faculty work as the traditional distinctions among research, teaching, and service (Colbeck, 1998).

Faculty tend to allocate more time and attention to the tasks they believe are most closely evaluated (Dornbusch, 1979). If they believe that the evaluation of research has the most impact on their rewards, for example, they will spend more time on research at the expense of other scholarly activities. Similarly, service, variously called outreach (Lynton, 1995), the scholarship of application (Boyer, 1990), or the scholarship of engagement (Checkoway, 2001), is often perceived as distinct from and less important than research or teaching; therefore, faculty devote less time to this domain (Ward, 2003).

The most innovative and vulnerable faculty may be particularly susceptible to the dangers of depicting their work in ways that differ from conventional separate categories. Even when a college or university has reconsidered scholarship along the lines advocated by Boyer (1990), assistant professors find it necessary to communicate their academic accomplishments in separate research, teaching, and service categories in their promotion and tenure dossiers. Huber (2004) compares experiences of junior faculty engaged in chemistry education in two universities. One chemist allocated his many integrated activities into the traditional categories recognized by his university and secured tenure with ease. The other initially "tore out the dividers still labeled 'teaching,' 'research,' and 'service' and reorganized her material to emphasize the integrated nature of her work" (Huber, 2004, p. 5). Although her university had recently emphasized the integration of academic work, this chemist was promoted only after she separated her academic accomplishments to fit the conventional categories.

Separation of academic work into distinct categories also risks its devolution into bureaucratic division of labor. Complex work can be managed by dividing tasks among individuals who specialize in one area (Scott, 2003). An ever increasing proportion of faculty have teaching as their primary or sole responsibility, and most of them are ineligible for tenure (Gappa, 2000). Tenure track faculty, especially at research and doctoral-granting universities, experience ever more pressure to spend most of their time on discovery and publication. As faculty spend less time on service or the scholarship of application, nonfaculty student affairs and outreach professionals have assumed more responsibility for performance of college and university community service obligations. Perhaps because faculty do not have enough time to accomplish the many demands of each separate domain of their work satisfactorily (Fairweather, 2002), academic labor is being subdivided among various specialized workers who are increasingly managed by administrators and thereby deprofessionalized (Rhoades, 1998).

Public Scholarship Reintegrates the Domains of Academic Work

Academic work need not be subdivided. While bureaucratic organizational structures deal with complexity by subdividing labor, a professional model for organization relies on the performance of highly educated, flexible, complex workers who are able to handle nonroutine problems independently and draw on their expertise to make connections across different elements of their work (Scott, 2003). Individual faculty may conduct academic work in an integrated way, using their research to inform their teaching, their service and teaching as sources of ideas for their research, and their teaching as opportunities to provide service to the community as well as foster student learning. Judith Ramaley, now in her third university presidency, asserts that "it is possible to blend" all domains of "intellectual activity into a distinctive whole" (2000, p. 11).

Empirical research shows that as faculty enact their work on a daily basis, they often engage in tasks that combine two or more domains, whether the domains are labeled "research, teaching, and service," "discovery, application, integration, and teaching" (Boyer, 1990), or "discovery, learning, and engagement" (Kellogg Commission, 2000). In two studies involving daily observations of faculty, Colbeck (1998, 2004) documented that twenty-five assistant, associate, and full professors of English, chemistry, and physics accomplished teaching and research purposes simultaneously between 8 and 34 percent of the time they devoted to work activities.

Public scholarship involves faculty accomplishing academic work in a way that integrates service/application/engagement with discovery/research and teaching/learning. According to Jeremy Cohen (2001), associate vice provost for undergraduate education at The Pennsylvania State University, "Public scholarship is a means of conceptually organizing the way we think about the integration of civic participation, research, and general and domain based discovery through teaching and learning" (p. 242).

Public scholarship is not a separate faculty role, so does not add further demands to an already overworked faculty. Instead, public scholarship *is* academic work, reframed as a unified whole, enabling faculty members to accomplish multiple scholarship goals simultaneously and thereby improving the overall efficiency and effectiveness of their academic work. The following conditions for public scholarship are essential (adapted from Glassick, Huber, and Maeroff, 1997):

Faculty, students, and community members together identify clear goals and research questions for inquiry into a problem that addresses a real-world issue.
The inquiry is grounded in a thorough review of relevant prior research.
Appropriate investigative methods are used for systematic inquiry that addresses the research questions.
The results of the inquiry are presented in a form suitable for review and critique by peers of the faculty, students, and community members.
Faculty, students, and community members have opportunities together and separately to reflect on the contribution of their efforts to their own and one another's learning and to the ideal of developing and sharing knowledge as a public good.

Public Scholarship at The Pennsylvania State University

A growing group of faculty and administrators at Penn State are conducting public scholarship, approaching their work as professionals who integrate all scholarly domains. Originating in 1999 with five faculty led by Jeremy Cohen, the Public Scholarship Associates articulated a set of goals to recruit other faculty, create opportunities for meaningful participation, develop a center to foster public scholarship, and share public scholarship in ways that recognize faculty members' integrated scholarly contributions.

Within two years, the number of Public Scholarship Associates had grown to forty faculty from geography, philosophy, electrical engineering, rural sociology, political science, communications, and higher education departments. Small grants funded by various campus offices and the Pennsylvania Campus Compact were offered to faculty who incorporated public scholarship into their undergraduate courses. Awardees also became Public Scholarship Associates.

The group meets several times each semester to interact with community representatives, plan an undergraduate minor in civic engagement, and explore the meaning and practice of public scholarship, along with undergraduate poster exhibitions and day-long seminars on public scholarship. "The creation of Public Scholarship Associates bestowed a sense of institutional legitimacy to the people who are striving to broaden a grass roots constituency for promoting public scholarship, both within the university and beyond" (Cohen and Yapa, 2003, p. 7).

Public Scholarship Associates at Penn State find ways to integrate all domains of their work. Examples of public scholarship in psychology, geography, and architectural engineering show how faculty enrich their teaching with their research, inform their research with lessons learned from the community, and involve their students in research with community partners for the benefit of the public good (Colbeck, 2002).

Psychology as Public Scholarship. Children and adolescents' development of social competence is the focus of Jeffrey Parker's discovery/research. This associate professor of psychology investigates friendship, loneliness, and bullying behaviors among middle school students. Parker also teaches an undergraduate course focused on adolescent social competence (Parker and Walker, 2003). In the course, undergraduates work in teams to provide local middle school students with workshops on social skills, bullying, and school violence. In weekly sessions with Parker, undergraduate participants review and critique the theories and research about factors that place children at risk and about effective interventions. They also present their proposed workshops to get feedback from Parker and their peers before presenting them to the middle school students. Undergraduates in the practicum engage in scholarship as they write process notes, relate their experiences in schools to relevant literature, and prepare case study analyses of the needs and progress of particular children, which are available for review by their peers and Parker.

Parker's research informs his teaching of the course, but the experiences of the undergraduates also inform his research. Parker acknowledges that ideas learned from his undergraduate colleagues provide new ideas and insights for his own discovery and publications, which are often coauthored with students (see, for example, Parker, Low, Walker, and Biggs, 2005). Parker has also received funding from the National Science Foundation for his public scholarship course.

Three principles guide Parker's public scholarship. First, the focus is on serious intellectual engagement rather than on volunteerism. Second, the learning goal is improving students' understanding of how "rigorous scientific inquiry can inform efforts to improve children's lives, and vice versa" (Parker and Walker, 2003, p. 19). Third, the service is designed to be sustained and to improve children's lives. A recent evaluation of the project in the schools showed that more than 90 percent of the 180 middle school students involved in the intervention program found it helpful.

Public Scholarship to Address Causes of Poverty. Lakshman Yapa, professor of geography, announces on his Web site that his current research project "is an academic program that integrates research, teaching, and service learning in West Philadelphia" (Yapa, 2005). Weaving together theories of economics, postmodern discourse, and geographical information systems (GIS), Yapa argues that economic solutions fail to address poverty. Yapa works with undergraduate and graduate students who participate in his project and course for academic credit, "Rethinking Urban Poverty." During summers in West Philadelphia, they work with neighborhood residents to explore causes of poor nutrition, quality of life, and ill health. Commuting costs, for example, depend on the geographical distribution of residences and jobs, available modes of transport, and insurance rates. Finding ways to reduce transport costs of inner-city residents becomes a way to increase their effective income. Improving the sense of personal agency for students and neighborhood residents is a goal of Yapa's integrated work. He asserts that "while public scholarship and service learning benefit the community, they also help the university tremendously by producing a different kind of graduate capable of critical thinking with a high sense of civic responsibility" (Yapa, 2003, p. 51). Yapa encourages students to use their specialized academic competencies to serve the community in ways that are proportionate to their power. In addition to Yapa's own recent publications on geography, globalization, and poverty, his project Web site includes publicly available evidence of students' scholarship: their abstracts of projects on topics ranging from computer mapping of neighborhood resources to community nursing centers to street poetry and music.

Engineering for Sustainability. Public scholarship for architectural engineer David Riley involves green building, sustainability, environmental awareness, and engineering education. This associate professor brings industry experience and a commitment to sustainable living to his work as an integrated professional. Riley's American Indian Housing Initiative (AIHI) involves a partnership with Chief Dull Knife College of the Northern Cheyenne Nation. Undergraduate and graduate students participate in a year-long three-part program. A spring lecture course combines information about American Indian culture, history, and sociopolitics with information about sustainable building technologies (Grommes and Riley, 2004). During the summer, students collaborate with tribal members to build a green home or community building on the reservation in Montana using straw bale construction, including a center for the general equivalency diploma program, a technology center, and a day care center for the college. Informal feedback from the Northern Cheyenne includes expressions of gratitude for the partnership, especially because the AIHI group returns every summer, unlike other research teams.

A concluding fall semester course engages students and instructors in critical reflection on the summer experience and on future application of sustainable technologies for the Northern Cheyenne and themselves. Riley is engaged in an intensive scholarship of teaching effort to understand how public scholarship about sustainability affects learning for students, instructors, and tribal members. He has presented peer-reviewed results of his scholarly inquiry into this community teaching effort at national and international conferences (Grommes and Riley, 2004; Riley, 2004). He is working with engineering colleagues at Penn State and other universities to explore the relationship between public scholarship and sustainability education and other community partners. In addition, Riley publishes results of research conducted about the construction in engineering and education journals.

Interdisciplinary Collaboration: The Enfranchisement Project. Public Scholarship Associates at Penn State have also fostered interdisciplinary collaboration. During 2001, several faculty and graduate students met informally and regularly to explore issues of voter enfranchisement. Led by Jeremy Cohen, a professor of communications as well as associate vice provost of undergraduate education, six faculty engaged their students and one another in efforts to examine the processes that developed as Pennsylvania voters went to the polls for the 2000 U.S. presidential election.

Early in spring semester, faculty in communications (Richard Barton), political science (Robert O'Connor), agriculture extension and education (Constance Flanagan), geography (Lakshman Yapa), and higher education (Carol Colbeck) met with Cohen to explore creative approaches to fostering students' civic understanding while improving participative democracy. The faculty shared information about their courses and considered how to involve students in public scholarship projects about enfranchisement. Students in Yapa's course learned GIS by mapping Pennsylvania counties by size, ethnicity, age, and income level of the population. In O'Connor's political science course, undergraduate students contacted officials in each county to ascertain the voting method used and percentage of overvotes (more than one candidate selected for a single office) and undervotes (no candidate clearly selected) for president. Students in the introductory communications course supervised by Barton learned about media effects by studying the role of newspapers, television, and the Internet on the progress and outcomes of the 2000 election. Doctoral students in Flanagan's course on youth civic engagement developed and administered a survey to students in the introductory communications course to investigate the effect of the unit on students' perceptions of media use and consequent development of a sense of responsibility regarding the democratic process and presidential elections. The doctoral students presented their findings at an international conference (Moses and Wharton Michael, 2003).

Faculty working on the enfranchisement project offered each other feedback about their course designs and provided helpful literature and resource person contact information. They also explored connections between their individual discipline-based public scholarship endeavors. A graduate student working with Yapa, for example, used GIS methods to map the information gained from O'Connor's class about voting methods and patterns of over- and undervoting across Pennsylvania counties. The group discussed publishing the results of their interdisciplinary efforts but did not, in part because the events of September 11, 2001, overwhelmed attention to other civic engagement issues and in part because the faculty members felt they needed to retreat to their own department to fulfill disciplinary responsibilities. Nevertheless, the enfranchisement project demonstrated how faculty engaged in public scholarship made connections across disciplines as well as between the various domains of their academic work, thereby enhancing their discovery, application, integration, and teaching and their students' learning.

Evaluating and Rewarding Public Scholarship

Public scholarship at Penn State shows how the different domains of academic work can be integrated and how the resulting products can and should be even more intellectually rigorous than discovery, application, or teaching by themselves. More remains to be done, however, to recognize, evaluate, and reward public scholarship as wholly integrated and intellectually rigorous academic work. According to Ramaley (2000), "Definitions of faculty work incorporated into faculty promotion and tenure guidelines [should] reflect sufficient breadth to recognize work that is community-based, interdisciplinary, and collaborative. Broadening the concepts of scholarly work will be extremely difficult unless a campus devises credible and effective ways to document and evaluate all forms of scholarship and a broad range of pedagogies" (p. 13).

An original goal of Penn State's Public Scholarship Associates was "the sharing of public scholarship teaching, research, and service within our own academic community in ways that recognize its scholarly basis for purposes of professional development as well as for tenure and promotion and salary recognition of performance" (Cohen and Yapa, 2003, p. 6). At Penn State, as at most other colleges and universities, faculty are still evaluated as if the different domains of their work are entirely separate. For annual reviews and promotion and tenure dossiers, faculty must document research publications, presentations, and grants in one section; teaching courses, advising students, and course development in another section; and service to institution, profession, and the community in a third section. There are early signs of recognizing the integrated complexity of faculty work, however. Penn State promotion and tenure forms were recently amended to include in the research section "description of outreach or other activities in which there was significant use of candidate's expertise."

Integrated academic work—public scholarship—should be subject to the same scholarly review that Glassick, Huber, and Maeroff (1997) advocate for each separate domain of academic work. Public scholarship should have clear goals, adequate preparation, appropriate methods, significant results, effective presentation, and reflective critique. External evaluators and promotion and tenure committees should be able to see evidence of original and creative contribution to knowledge, peer and client review, demonstrated effectiveness, and broad dissemination (O'Meara, 2002). The documents that faculty prepare for evaluation should indicate the ways and the extent to which each domain of their work informs and reinforces the others (Colbeck, 2002). Faculty might also explain how their discovery/ research informs course work that responds to both students' and community members' needs or how their application/service contributes to research by addressing current and important social, political, economic, or environmental issues.

Implications for Institutional Research

Institutional researchers may wish to collect and analyze data about public scholarship in terms of faculty workload, faculty productivity, or student learning. Many institutions currently collect faculty workload information in average hours per week or percentage of time allocated to the mutually exclusive categories of teaching, research, and service. Combining Boyer's four domains with a public scholarship approach, such forms might be modified to elicit information about allocation of time solely to discovery, integration, application, and teaching as well as how much of each faculty member's time is allocated to two or more domains at the same time. For example, faculty might be asked to document the extent to which the time they spent on teaching also advanced development of new knowledge (discovery) or contributed to community development (application). With this information, institutional researchers could assess the extent to which faculty members accomplish more than one academic goal at the same time (Colbeck, 1998, 2002).

There may need to be only minor changes in the way institutions account for faculty productivity. Examples provided by Jeffrey Parker, Lakshman Yapa, and David Riley show that public scholarship results in external funding and refereed publications and presentations about the disciplinary research as well as scholarship of teaching in well-respected journals, disciplinary conferences, and academic presses, as with any other scholarship. Faculty also produce student credit hours for the courses taught that incorporate disciplinary-based learning in service with the community. Institutional researchers may account for one additional aspect of faculty productivity that results from public scholarship: number and depth of relationships with community partners. Records and accounts of university-community partnerships that foster discovery, integration, application, and teaching may well enhance town-gown relations.

Institutional researchers may wish to investigate the extent to which participation in public scholarship enhances student learning of disciplinary knowledge and fosters attitudes and actions indicative of active participation in democracy. They could compare student learning outcomes for students in public scholarship courses with those in traditional lecture courses and active learning courses that do not have a community engagement component. Researchers might accomplish these goals by adding new questions to the rating forms students complete about courses at the end of each term, or they may design separate surveys to collect these data from students.

Conclusion

Public scholarship enables faculty, students, and community members to work together to define real-world problems in all their complexity and then to cooperate on the process of addressing those problems. Reframing academic work as public scholarship fosters faculty engagement in and administrator and peer evaluation of professional work as an integrated whole that is more than the sum of its parts. Faculty who conduct public scholarship view their discovery, integration, application, and teaching scholarships as a complex and interrelated public resource that leads to publication-worthy discovery while also actively engaging students in meaningful learning with real-world problems in partnership with the community outside academe (Cohen, 2001).

The more that organizational evaluations encourage faculty to envision and document their academic work as an integrated whole, the more individual faculty will have personal goals for their work consistent with public scholarship, feel capable of conducting public scholarship, and believe that their work context is supportive of their engagement in public scholarship. Consequently, faculty whose work is evaluated as an integrated whole are more likely than those whose work is evaluated in separate domains to engage in more public scholarship more often.

References

Boyer, E. L. *Scholarship Reconsidered: Priorities of the Professoriate.* Princeton, N.J.: Carnegie Foundation for the Advancement of Teaching, 1990.

Braxton, J. J., Luckey, W., and Helland, P. *Institutionalizing a Broader View of Scholarship Through Boyer's Four Domains.* ASHE-ERIC Higher Education Report, vol. 29, no. 2. San Francisco: Jossey-Bass, 2002.

Checkoway, B. "Renewing the Civic Mission of the American Research University." *Journal of Higher Education,* 2001, 72(2), 125–147.

Cohen, J. "Public Scholarship: Serving to Learn." In M. E. Kenny, L. K. Simon, K. Kiley-Bradeck, and R. M. Lerner (eds.), *Learning to Serve: Promoting Civil Society Through Service Learning* (pp. 235–255). Norwood, Mass.: Kluwer, 2001.

Cohen, J., and Yapa, L. "Introduction." In J. Cohen and L. Yapa (eds.), *A Blueprint for Public Scholarship at Penn State*. University Park, Pa.: Penn State, 2003.

Colbeck, C. L. "Merging in a Seamless Blend: How Faculty Integrate Teaching and Research." *Journal of Higher Education*, 1998, 69(6), 647–671.

Colbeck, C. "Integration: Evaluating Faculty Work as a Whole." In C. L. Colbeck (ed.), *Evaluating Faculty Performance*. New Directions for Institutional Research, no. 114. San Francisco: Jossey-Bass, 2002.

Colbeck, C. L. "A Cybernetic Systems Model of Teaching and Research Production: Impact of Disciplinary Differences." Paper presented at the International Colloquium on Research and Teaching: Closing the Divide? Southampton, U.K., 2004.

Dornbusch, S. M. "Perspectives from Sociology: Organizational Evaluation of Faculty Performances." In D. R. Lewis and W. E. Becker Jr. (eds.), *Academic Rewards in Higher Education*. Cambridge, Mass.: Ballinger, 1979.

Fairweather, J. S. "The Mythologies of Faculty Productivity: Implications for Institutional Policy and Decision Making." *Journal of Higher Education*, 2002, 73(1), 26–48.

Gappa, J. M. "The New Faculty Majority: Somewhat Satisfied But Not Eligible for Tenure." In L. S. Hagedorn (ed.), *What Contributes to Job Satisfaction Among Faculty and Staff*. New Directions for Higher Education, no. 105. San Francisco: Jossey-Bass, 2000.

Glassick, C. E., Huber, M. T., and Maeroff, G. I. *Scholarship Assessed: Evaluation of the Professoriate*. San Francisco: Jossey-Bass, 1997.

Grommes, A., and Riley, D. R. "Learning from Native Cultures: Educational Opportunities in Sustainability, Cultural Sensitivity, and Global Awareness." Paper presented at the annual meeting of the American Society for Engineering Education, Salt Lake City, Utah, June 2004.

Huber, M. T. *Balancing Acts: The Scholarship of Teaching and Learning in Academic Careers*. Washington, D.C.: American Association for Higher Education and Carnegie Foundation for the Advancement of Teaching, 2004.

Hutchings, P., and Schulman, L. S. "The Scholarship of Teaching: New Elaborations, New Developments." *Change*, 1999, 31(5), 10–15.

Kellogg Commission on the Future of State and Land-Grant Universities. *Renewing the Covenant: Learning, Discovery, and Engagement in a New Age and a Different World*. Washington, D.C.: National Association of State Universities and Land Grant Colleges, 2000. [http://www.nasulgc.org/publications/Kellogg/Kellogg2000_covenant.pdf]. Accessed June 15, 2005.

Lynton, E. A. *Making the Case for Professional Service*. Washington, D.C.: American Association for Higher Education, 1995.

Moses, N., and Wharton Michael, P. J. "The Enfranchisement Project: The Impact of a Case Study Intervention and Media Use on Perception of Responsibility to Community." Poster session at the annual meeting of the International Communication Association, San Diego, Calif., 2003.

O'Meara, K. A. "Uncovering the Values in Faculty Evaluation of Service as Scholarship." *Journal of Higher Education*, 2002, 26(1), 57–80.

Parker, J. G., Low, C., Walker, A. R., and Biggs, B. A. "Children's Friendship Jealousy: Assessment of Individual Differences and Links to Sex, Self-Esteem, Aggression, and Social Adjustment." *Developmental Psychology*, 2005, 41, 235–250.

Parker, J. G., and Walker, A. R. "Encouraging Adolescent Social Competence: A Practicum." In J. Cohen and L. Yapa (eds.), *A Blueprint for Public Scholarship at Penn State*. University Park, Pa.: Penn State, 2003.

Ramaley, J. A. "Embracing Civic Responsibility." *AAHE Bulletin*, 2000, 52, 9–13.

Rhoades, G. *Managed Professionals: Unionized Faculty and Restructuring Academic Labor*. Albany: State University of New York Press, 1998.

Riley, D. R. "Educational Challenges of Sustainable Construction." CIB World Building Congress, Toronto, Canada, May 2004.

Scott, W. R. *Organizations: Rational, Natural, and Open Systems.* (5th ed.) Upper Saddle River, N.J.: Prentice Hall, 2003.

Ward, K. *Faculty Service Roles and the Scholarship of Engagement.* ASHE-ERIC Higher Education Report, vol. 29, no. 5. San Francisco: Jossey-Bass, 2003.

Yapa, L. "Rethinking Urban Poverty: The Philadelphia Field Project." In J. Cohen and L. Yapa (eds.), *A Blueprint for Public Scholarship at Penn State.* University Park, Pa.: Penn State, 2003.

Yapa, L. "Lakshman Yapa." Retrieved June 15, 2005, from http://www.geog.psu.edu/people/yapa.

Yapa, L. "Public Scholarship in the Postmodern University." In R. A. Eberly and J. Cohen (eds.), *A Laboratory for Public Scholarship and Democracy.* New Directions for Teaching and Learning, no. 105. San Francisco: Jossey-Bass, 2006.

CAROL L. COLBECK is director of the Center for the Study of Higher Education and an associate professor of higher education at The Pennsylvania State University.

PATTY WHARTON MICHAEL is a doctoral candidate in the College of Communications at The Pennsylvania State University.

2

This chapter examines the construct scholarship of teaching and learning using a Parsonian four-function paradigm that serves as an analytical structure for organizing and examining some of the key issues in the emerging literature.

Exploring the Dimensions of the Scholarship of Teaching and Learning: Analytics for an Emerging Literature

Michael B. Paulsen, Kenneth A. Feldman

With the publication of *Scholarship Reconsidered,* Boyer (1990) presented a perspective on the multidimensionality of the construct of scholarship—the dimensions being discovery, integration, application, and teaching—that has since stimulated a good deal of reflection, conversation, research, and writing. He maintained that "the time has come to move beyond the tired old 'teaching versus research' debate and give the familiar and honorable term 'scholarship' a broader, more capacious meaning, one that brings legitimacy to the full scope of academic work" (p. 16). This statement offered potential comfort to many faculty who had long felt uncomfortable with the ongoing disparity in academe between rewards for teaching and those for research. However, Boyer's explanations of the meanings of each of the four dimensions of scholarship he proposed were uneven, and among the dimensions, he offered the least clarification about the meaning of the scholarship of teaching. In an apparent response to this absence of guidance from Boyer, coupled with a persistent confidence in the potential fruitfulness of this construct, a number of theoretical and empirical inquiries into the nature of the scholarship of teaching and learning (SoTL) have appeared in an emerging literature.

Yet in spite of various insightful efforts, the SoTL construct continues to elude complete consistency, clarity, and consensus (Huber and Hutchings, 2005; Kreber, 2001). In fact, Braxton, Luckey, and Helland (2002) describe the ensuing debate in the scholarship of teaching and learning literature as a "conceptual quagmire" (p. 106).

In considering the challenge of clarifying the SoTL construct, we extend our previous work (Paulsen and Feldman, 2003), which used the Parsonian four-function paradigm to identify and investigate the nature of each of the requisite subsystems of the SoTL human action system. We use this four-part model as a heuristic device to explore what we view as the four primary dimensions of the SoTL construct, employing the model as an analytical structure for clarifying, organizing, and examining some of the key issues in the emerging literature on the SoTL construct and for developing an inventory of examples for each of these dimensions.

The SoTL System: An Application of the Four-Function Paradigm

The four-function paradigm is a well-established analytical framework developed by Talcott Parsons and other sociologists to identify, describe, and analyze the four functional dimensions of human action in social, economic, evolutionary, political, and educational systems (see Parsons and Platt, 1973; Parsons and Smelser, 1956; Munch, 1987). We have previously used this paradigm as an analytical framework to identify and articulate the four functional subsystems of the overall scholarship action system—research and graduate training, teaching, service, and academic citizenship (Paulsen and Feldman, 1995b)—as well as to investigate in depth the more specific SoTL action system, which itself is one of the four functional subsystems of the overall scholarship action system (Paulsen and Feldman, 2003).

The four-function paradigm provides a set of uniform criteria for differentiating and classifying system actions into subsystems by specifying which of the four functions each action performs. In this chapter, as earlier (Paulsen and Feldman, 2003), we use the four functional imperatives—pattern maintenance, adaptation, goal attainment, and integration—and the distinguishing characteristics and features of actions performing each of the four separate functions to make reasonable decisions about which kinds of scholarly faculty activities perform each of the requisite functions in the SoTL system (see Figure 2.1). The scholarly work of faculty in the SoTL system is defined here as those, *and only those,* faculty activities that directly relate to their specialized fields of knowledge or expertise. The nature of this knowledge for the SoTL system is examined in the next section on the pattern maintenance function of the SoTL system.

Figure 2.1. Scholarship of Teaching and Learning System

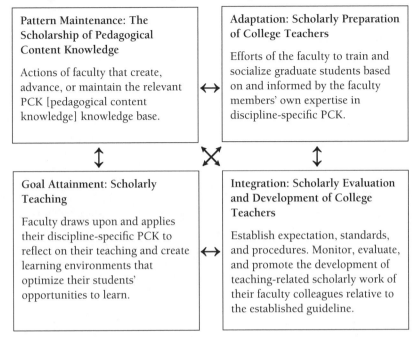

Pattern Maintenance: The Scholarship of Pedagogical Content Knowledge

The symbolic frame of reference essential to the SoTL system's performance of the pattern maintenance function—and one that informs scholarly work in all subsystems of the SoTL system—is the knowledge base for teaching and learning. What, then, is the nature of this essential knowledge base for teaching and learning? A growing number of scholars emphasize the central role of the disciplines—the source of content knowledge for teaching and learning—in models of the SoTL (Huber and Morreale, 2002; Hutchings and Clarke, 2004; McKinney, 2004). In fact, it was the recognition of the content-based differences or domain specificity of pedagogy that led Shulman (2002) "to invent the concept of pedagogical content knowledge, the idea that teaching is itself domain and subject specific" (p. vi). Consistent with prior work in the SoTL literature (Braxton, Luckey, and Helland, 2002; Paulsen, 2001; Rice, 1991; Shulman, 2002), we view pedagogical content knowledge as a key feature of the knowledge base for teaching and learning. In his classic work identifying the components of the knowledge base for teaching, Shulman (1987) explains that "pedagogical content knowledge is of special interest because it identifies the distinctive bodies of knowledge for teaching. It represents the blending of content and pedagogy into an understanding of how particular topics, problems, or issues are organized, represented, and adapted to the diverse interests and abilities of learners, and presented for instruction" (p. 8).

Our view of the distinctive knowledge base for teaching and learning is similar, but not identical, to that of Shulman. We use the term *pedagogical content knowledge* (PCK) to refer to the knowledge base for teaching and learning, and we explicitly conceptualize the PCK construct as a synthesis of pedagogical knowledge (PK) and academic content (disciplinary) knowledge (CK). We view those actions of faculty that create, advance, or maintain the relevant PCK knowledge base as performing the pattern maintenance function of the SoTL system, and we identify this subsystem as the scholarship of pedagogical content knowledge (Paulsen, 2001). In particular, when faculty action adds to or advances the PCK knowledge base, it constitutes an act of scholarship and serves to increase the essential resources that inform scholarly work and promote meaningful communication across all four SoTL subsystems. This view of the functional purpose of action in this subsystem is congruent with Braxton, Luckey, and Helland's view (2002) that the "goal of the scholarship of teaching should be the development and improvement of pedagogical content knowledge" (p. 106).

But what criteria or characteristics of the advances in the PCK knowledge base identify, define, and distinguish them as acts of scholarship in the SoTL system? In his widely cited article "Teaching as Community Property" (1993), Shulman explains that "scholarship entails an artifact, a *product,* some form of community property that can be shared, discussed, critiqued, exchanged, built upon. So, if pedagogy is to become an important part of scholarship, we have to provide it with this same kind of documentation and transformation. . . . [and] the artifacts of teaching must be created and preserved so that they can be judged by communities of peers beyond the office next door" (p. 7, emphasis added). Consistent with this view of scholarship, a growing number of scholars now explicitly articulate the SoTL construct in terms of "products" that document or present the scholarship in "forms" that others can indeed critique, exchange, and build on (Braxton, Luckey, and Helland, 2002; Hutchings and Shulman, 1999; McKinney, 2004; Richlin, 2001). Concurring with the approach of these scholars, we view such SoTL products as the acts of faculty scholarship that serve to expand the knowledge base for teaching and learning—that is, the relevant PCK knowledge base for each scholar's field (Paulsen, 2001).

In practice, a variety of products of faculty work could be appropriately documented in forms that would meet all of these criteria that define them as acts of teaching and learning scholarship—what Nelson (2003) refers to as "genres of SoTL"—and could thereby be added to the relevant PCK knowledge base. Examples of professional activities of faculty that would constitute action in this subsystem are given in the chapter appendix.

Disciplinary contexts are important in understanding the development of SoTL products. "Each field brings its own questions, methods, and rules of evidence to this work, and faculty are much more likely to embrace (or at least to understand) the work if it reflects the culture and character of the field" (Hutchings and Clarke, 2004, p. 173). In their examination of the experiences of participants in the SoTL programs initiated by the Carnegie Academy for the Scholarship of Teaching and Learning (CASTL), Huber and Morreale (2002) explore how SoTL is situated and how it is variously produced within and across disciplinary boundaries. The social science disciplines are characterized by conceptual frameworks that clearly connect to the study of teaching and learning phenomena and by quantitative and qualitative methods of inquiry that are well suited to such investigation. For example, cognitive psychologists examine information processing during learning; sociologists consider issues of race, class, gender, and group behavior in learning environments; and communication experts analyze teaching as acts of communication. In the natural sciences, well-established science education communities productively use social science methods to study teaching and learning in their fields. Some teaching and learning scholars have even reached across disciplines to generate SoTL products (see Calder, Cutler, and Kelly, 2002; Huber and Morreale, 2002).

Adaptation: Scholarly Preparation of College Teachers

Performance of the adaptation function for the SoTL system requires recruiting and training future faculty—graduate students who plan academic careers—as scholars of teaching and learning in a discipline or interdisciplinary field of expertise and socializing them to the discipline-specific PCK that will inform all their work in the role of teaching scholar. When the efforts of faculty to train and socialize graduate students are based on and informed by these faculty members' own expertise in discipline-specific PCK, their efforts constitute scholarly work in the performance of the adaptation function of the SoTL system; that is, they are engaged in the scholarly preparation of future faculty as teachers.

The socialization of graduate students is a complex process providing many opportunities for faculty to contribute to graduate students' assimilation of the PCK knowledge base of their discipline. Some of the campus-based programs of the CASTL have explicitly focused on the role of SoTL in graduate education (Hutchings and Clarke, 2004). For example, the faculty in the sociology department at Indiana University require their graduate students to take a sequence of courses on teaching and learning, one of which requires a SoTL project in which students recently used "the various methods of the discipline (ethnographic study, in-depth interviews, record analysis, and other approaches) to study an experimental pilot program designed to reengineer the IU first-year experience" (p. 168). This example illustrates how faculty can work to socialize graduate students to their discipline's PCK in terms of both the content and the methods of the discipline.

In addition, a growing number of departments offer courses, seminars, or colloquia on teaching and learning in their disciplines, and these components of graduate programs increasingly include a SoTL perspective (Hutchings and Clarke, 2004; Robinson and Nelson, 2003), offering further evidence that faculty are productively engaged in scholarly work related to the socialization of graduate students to the PCK of their disciplines. Finally, Shulman's recommendations (2004) of how campuses can best support the SoTL include locating a university's teaching academy in the graduate school itself, so that just as members of the graduate faculty have traditionally served as mentors guiding their students in their research, graduate faculty might now also serve as mentors guiding their students in their development as scholars of teaching and learning. In this way, doctoral students will be viewed as future stewards of not only the CK but also the PCK of their disciplines.

In sum, faculty work that constitutes action in this subsystem, informed as it is by the expertise of faculty members in their own discipline-specific PCK, socializes graduate students to that PCK knowledge base, thereby preparing these students for their future scholarly work as teachers. Examples of such professional activities of faculty are given in the chapter appendix.

Goal Attainment: Scholarly Teaching

Performance of the goal attainment function for the SoTL system occurs when faculty draw on and apply their discipline-specific PCK to reflect on their teaching and create learning environments that optimize their students' opportunities to learn. The functional purpose of action in this subsystem is thus "the development and improvement of pedagogical practices," as noted by Braxton, Luckey, and Helland (2002, p. 106). We label actions of faculty in this subsystem as "scholarly teaching." College teachers, like many other professionals, have long been viewed as reflective practitioners in the instructional improvement and related literature (Kreber and Cranton, 2000; Paulsen and Feldman, 1995a). Indeed, the SoTL literature provides consistent support for the view that neither the process (scholarly teaching) nor the product (scholarship of teaching and learning) interpretations of teaching and learning scholarship would be possible without reflection by the teacher. When reflective teaching is informed by the knowledge base for teaching and learning, the result represents what many in the SoTL literature conceptualize as scholarly teaching (Hutchings and Shulman, 1999; McKinney, 2004; Richlin, 2001). For example, Hutchings and Shulman (1999) explain that when teaching entails "certain practices of classroom assessment and evidence gathering, when it is informed not only by the latest ideas in the field but by current ideas about teaching the field, when it invites peer collaboration and review, *then* that teaching might rightly be called scholarly or reflective, or informed" (p. 13, emphasis in original). In this statement, Hutchings and Shulman clearly use *reflective* and *informed* as synonyms for *scholarly* in order to define *scholarly teaching*.

Faculty work that constitutes action in the subsystem of scholarly teaching is informed by and applies faculty members' expertise in their own discipline-specific PCK to create effective learning environments and promote student learning. Examples of such professional activities of faculty are given in the chapter appendix.

Contributors to the SoTL literature have become more consistent and explicit in making a substantive distinction between scholarly teaching and the scholarship of teaching and learning (McKinney, 2004; Richlin and Cox, 2004; Robinson and Nelson, 2003). This distinction is important for understanding the nature of different types of scholarly work performed by faculty in the SoTL action system. *Scholarly teaching* encompasses those teaching behaviors that are informed by the appropriate discipline-specific knowledge base of PCK and perform the goal attainment function of the SoTL system by promoting student learning, but are insufficient by themselves to produce additions to the PCK knowledge base; the *scholarship of teaching and learning* refers to faculty activities that are both informed by and produce additions to the PCK knowledge base, thereby performing the pattern maintenance function of the SoTL system.

Our analysis leads us to support the contention in the literature that the knowledge bases for teaching and learning that inform teachers in this reflective or scholarly teaching subsystem of action can include both research-based and experience-based knowledge (Kreber and Cranton, 2000). Addressing this issue, Weimer (2001) delineates various types of problems that must be addressed to identify, codify, report, and disseminate the wisdom of practice so that it can become part of the knowledge base of teaching and learning. She explains that the process of creating useful reports of effective practice for dissemination could be improved by embedding such practice in relevant conceptual frameworks, connecting these practices to existing empirical work, clarifying the contexts in which effective practice occurs (including historical perspectives when reporting practice), and viewing the wisdom of practice as valued knowledge that we have a responsibility to preserve and pass on. Thus, some faculty actions in the subsystem of reflective teaching might well initiate and subsequently lead to further actions by faculty that produce contributions to the relevant PCK knowledge base. Based on our analysis of the SoTL as an action system, those subsequent actions would perform the pattern maintenance function and would take place in the scholarship of pedagogical content knowledge subsystem.

Integration: Scholarly Evaluation and Development of College Teachers

Performance of the integration function for the SoTL system occurs when faculty use their discipline-specific PCK to guide their efforts to (1) establish expectations, standards, and procedures and (2) monitor, evaluate, and promote the development of teaching-related scholarly work of their faculty colleagues relative to those established guidelines. When faculty efforts to evaluate and develop the teaching-related scholarship of their colleagues are based on and informed by their expertise in discipline-specific PCK, their actions constitute scholarly work in this SoTL subsystem. Accordingly, we refer to the actions of faculty in the integration subsystem as scholarly evaluation and development of college teachers.

It is common to think of the evaluation of teaching as primarily based on student ratings. But when it comes to scholarly teaching and the scholarship of teaching and learning—both by definition grounded in the relevant PCK knowledge base—expertise in the field's PCK is required for the meaningful evaluation of either type of scholarly work. This means that evaluation of various forms of teaching and learning scholarship must be predominantly based on informed review by faculty colleagues. Scholars are only beginning to address the new issues and challenges that arise when trying to devise systems to provide meaningful evaluation of scholarly teaching and scholarship of teaching and learning (Braxton, Luckey, and Helland, 2002). For example, although most evaluation processes focus on traditionally conceived teaching effectiveness—which is not the same as scholarly teaching or scholarship of teaching and learning (Hutchings and Shulman, 1999)—and use rating forms that often neglect disciplinary differences in teaching (Paulsen, 2002), what constitutes scholarly teaching or scholarship of teaching and learning is highly dependent on the distinguishing characteristics of the disciplinary or interdisciplinary fields of study (Huber and Morreale, 2002; Shulman, 2002).

Important differences in disciplinary contexts—such as unique content, methods of inquiry, language, and the like—make establishing uniform sets of procedures for assessing the quality of various acts of teaching scholarship highly problematic. Nevertheless, some scholars have given us a place to start by developing some possible indicators of quality in teaching and learning scholarship (Theall and Centra, 2001). For example, Kreber and Cranton (2000) identify twenty-seven indicators of teaching scholarship; however, based on our own analysis of the SoTL as an action system, we would view their set of indicators as combining some activities that constitute the scholarship of teaching and learning (which subsumes scholarly teaching) with others that represent scholarly teaching alone. Braxton, Luckey, and Helland (2002) identify another substantial set of indicators of teaching and learning scholarship and arrange them in three categories—scholarly activities, unpublished scholarly outcomes, and publications—in an effort to distinguish between indicators of scholarly teaching and scholarship of teaching and learning.

Expectations about faculty work are usually viewed in terms of some allocation of effort among teaching, research, and service. But when faculty embrace the SoTL, the distinctions between the traditional categories of faculty work grow unclear, and scholars have to devise ways to translate the SoTL into existing forms of evaluation that clearly favor traditional research. "At the same time, committees must first agree to broaden the definition of scholarship used normally in their department and institution and then make a special effort to discern the degree of distinction of an unusual and often unfamiliar body of work" (Huber, 2004, p. 9). This type of committee work requires faculty to apply their own PCK expertise to inform their efforts to reshape the expectations, standards, norms, or procedures that will be used to evaluate the quality of scholarly teaching and scholarship of teaching and learning in their department. The faculty on this committee would be clearly engaged in scholarly evaluation and development and in performance of the integration function of the SoTL system.

Faculty development initiatives are also important in performing the integration function of the SoTL system, because they seek to improve teaching and promote conformity to conventional norms of instructional effectiveness or excellence in teaching (Paulsen and Feldman, 1995a). However, in the SoTL action system, of particular importance are faculty development initiatives that seek to advance the SoTL and promote conformity to new norms of quality in scholarly teaching and the scholarship of teaching and learning; the emerging literature now documents many exemplary programs of this nature at the national and campus levels (Cambridge, 2004; Robinson and Nelson, 2003). Finally, some scholars view growth in teaching and learning scholarship as a developmental process in faculty careers (Weston and McAlpine, 2001). Others have adapted and interpreted this model to explicitly represent a sequence of phases of development that starts with growth in effective teaching and leads to growth in scholarly teaching and eventually to growth in the SoTL. Within this framework, faculty learning communities have proven to be particularly effective in developing the teaching and learning scholarship of faculty and promoting conformity to new norms of quality in scholarly teaching and the scholarship of teaching and learning (Richlin and Cox, 2004).

In summary, faculty work that constitutes action in this subsystem is informed by and applies expertise of faculty members in their own discipline-specific PCK to establish teaching-related expectations, standards, and procedures and to monitor, evaluate, and promote the scholarly work of their faculty colleagues as teaching scholars. Professional activities of faculty related to the both the evaluation and development of teaching and learning scholarship are given in the chapter appendix.

SoTL as an Action System: Implications for Institutional Research and Policy

Offices of institutional research and other offices on campus that manage data (for example, offices of assessment and evaluation) often assess and prepare reports on the productivity and effectiveness of faculty members in their use of time devoted to teaching. Typical measures include faculty teaching loads, time spent on teaching and student contact hours, and students' and peers' ratings of teaching. Although these may be useful measures for assessing teaching through traditional lenses, they do not offer a particularly meaningful assessment of the productivity or effectiveness of faculty in the scholarship of teaching and learning. Because the SoTL movement is becoming more important on many campuses, institutional research officers (along with their colleagues in assessment and evaluation centers or campus teaching centers) are increasingly likely to be asked to support academic and administrative units in their efforts to meaningfully assess faculty work in the various aspects of teaching and learning scholarship.

In this context, using the Parsonian four-function paradigm to analyze faculty work in the SoTL action system has important implications for practice in institutional research and policy because it reveals multiple dimensions of faculty work in the area of teaching and learning scholarship. In particular, our analysis has identified and distinguished among four unique teaching-related action subsystems in which faculty may engage in scholarly activity. Understanding the nature and uniqueness of the kinds of faculty work that constitute scholarly activity in each of these subsystems provides a conceptual foundation for the construction of a practical inventory of teaching and learning scholarship—a SoTL inventory.

The conceptual framework for this inventory would include the four categories of scholarly faculty work, with each category corresponding to one of the four teaching-related action subsystems. For each category (or action subsystem), a fairly comprehensive list of teaching-related scholarly activities of faculty could be developed, starting, for example, with the listing of professional activities we present in the appendix as indicators of the scholarly work of faculty in each action subsystem. Although the underlying logic of the four-function paradigm is highly generalizable across academic domains, there would surely be some disciplinary differences in the concrete nature and description of various indicators in each category, as well as in the ways in which indicators would be documented in one's SoTL portfolio; careful attention would need to be paid to such differences.

If institutional researchers are successful in helping academic and administrative units develop a relatively comprehensive set of measures of faculty productivity and effectiveness in each of the four SoTL action subsystems, a number of important outcomes might result. In addition to traditional practices (or in some cases, even breaking with them), assessment of the productivity and effectiveness of faculty teaching would explicitly consider the scholarly aspects of teaching for the first time and would consider all four of the scholarly dimensions of teaching identified with the four-function paradigm. Such a multidimensional approach to assessment would draw meaningful attention to the breadth and depth of the scholarly work of faculty as they pursue the teaching mission of their institutions. At the very least, observers would have greater opportunities to understand that the work of faculty as teachers goes beyond the more limited perspective of good teaching as based, say, on student ratings or on visits of colleagues to a teacher's classroom. If done well, reports of assessments based on scholarly activity in all four SoTL subsystems would be more informative and presumably more satisfying for internal and external constituencies. For example, legislators, taxpayers, donors, and parents would have a much deeper understanding of the range of faculty activities that enhance students' learning opportunities. Likewise, academic and administrative units on campus, as well as governing board members, would have a greater opportunity to perceive that scholarly action of faculty in each of the four action subsystems is deserving of attention, visibility, recognition, credit, and reward. Promotion and tenure (and other personnel decisions) would be based on more complex documentation and insights into the scholarly work of faculty as teachers yet would also be more transparent because of the multidimensional approach to assessment of productivity and effectiveness. Finally, because scholarly action in all four of the SoTL subsystems is highly accessible to faculty at all types of traditional institutions—community colleges, liberal arts colleges, comprehensive colleges and universities, and doctoral/research universities—similarities in the nature of the scholarly work of faculty that contributes to an institution's teaching mission would be more apparent across institutional types.

SoTL as an Action System: Concluding Thoughts

We have used the Parsonian four-function paradigm as an analytical framework to identify and articulate the four functional subsystems of the scholarship of teaching and learning action system: scholarship of pedagogical content knowledge (PCK), scholarly preparation of college teachers, scholarly teaching, and scholarly evaluation and faculty development. Our application of this paradigm highlights the indispensability of the functions performed by all four subsystems. Action in the scholarship of pedagogical content knowledge subsystem advances PCK as the knowledge base for teaching and learning to inform action not only in its own subsystem but also in the three other subsystems. Action in the scholarly preparation of college teachers subsystem socializes future college teachers to the requisite PCK in order to advance teaching and learning scholarship over time. Action in the scholarly teaching subsystem pursues the goals of designing and implementing effective learning environments for students. Action in the scholarly evaluation and development subsystem develops appropriate expectations, norms, and standards for performance in scholarly teaching and the scholarship of teaching and learning and assesses the quality of performance in these areas.

In addition to illustrating the indispensability and uniqueness of action in each of the four subsystems, the application of the Parsonian paradigm also reveals some of the interconnections among the subsystems. First, action in the scholarship of pedagogical content knowledge subsystem is integral—and, in fact, is a prerequisite—to action in any of the other three subsystems of the overall SoTL action system. That is, although PCK is created and preserved by actions in the scholarship of pedagogical content knowledge subsystem, the scholarly action in each of the other three subsystems is informed by the relevant discipline-specific PCK knowledge base. Second, action in the scholarly preparation of college teachers subsystem is dedicated to socializing future faculty to the requisite PCK knowledge bases of their disciplines, which is necessary in order for scholarly action in the other subsystems to have continuity over time. Thus, if graduate students are socialized to the PCK knowledge base of their disciplines, when they themselves become faculty members they will be able to engage in scholarly teaching, scholarly evaluation and development, and the scholarship of pedagogical content knowledge. Third, some faculty actions in the scholarly teaching subsystem, such as using classroom assessment techniques, can initiate and subsequently lead to further faculty action in the scholarship of pedagogical content knowledge subsystem (thereby yielding SoTL products that contribute to the relevant PCK knowledge base). Fourth, action in the scholarly evaluation and development of college teachers subsystem involves faculty activities that evaluate and develop the quality of teaching and learning scholarship in all four subsystems. For instance, the efforts of department chairs or peers engaged in scholarly evaluation or development might help some teachers to improve their own scholarly teaching or create meaningful SoTL products. Future analyses might usefully explore additional interrelations and interdependencies among action in the four subsystems.

Appendix: Professional Activities Associated with the Four Functional Subsystems

Following are some examples of professional activities of faculty that would constitute action in each of the four functional subsystems. (Paulsen and Feldman, 2003, called these subsystems scholarship of pedagogical content knowledge, graduate training, reflective teaching, and faculty evaluation and development, respectively.)

- *Scholarship of pedagogical content knowledge:* Activities that produce such products as course or teaching portfolios; essays portraying examples of good practice, innovative ideas, expert knowledge from experimentation or self-reflection in one's own teaching; reports of classroom research and other quantitative or qualitative assessments or studies of key teaching-learning issues, changes in teaching practice, learning in different courses, sections, or institutions; descriptions of integration of research, theory, and practice; conference presentations or publications in disciplinary pedagogical journals

- *Scholarly preparation of college teachers:* Collaborating with graduate students on SoTL research projects; requiring these students to conduct discipline-specific pedagogical research; encouraging these students to use the content and methods of their own discipline to conduct SoTL projects; offering graduate courses on teaching the faculty members' own disciplines; encouraging teaching assistants to use classroom assessment techniques in their classes; designing assignments that require graduate students to become familiar with the publications in the pedagogical journals of their own disciplines; and conducting pedagogical colloquia in which graduate students participate

- *Scholarly teaching:* Applying existing research on student motivation to present academic content in ways that promote students' motivation to learn; applying existing research about the cognitive and behavioral learning strategies of students to design content-specific learning activities that promote students' use of effective learning strategies; using existing research knowledge about student diversity to develop a course or lectures in which disciplinary content is inclusive of the experiences of students who are diverse in terms of race, class, gender, and other characteristics; using classroom assessment techniques to discover what specific content students are or are not learning; implementing recommendations from the latest research on problem-based learning or cooperative learning strategies in designing activities to promote students' mastery of specialized disciplinary content; using reports of successful practice from one's disciplinary peers regarding effective teaching in the discipline (as given, say, in papers presented at conferences or in publications in the pedagogical journals of their own disciplines); and writing reflective essays—perhaps as part of course or teaching portfolios—that relate various sources of existing knowledge about teaching and learning to the special challenges of teaching the specialized content of one's own discipline

- *Scholarly evaluation and development of college teachers:* Scheduling a series of departmental or college-level faculty meetings to broaden the traditional definition of scholarship and reshape the expectations, standards, procedures, and indicators as components of systems to provide for meaningful evaluation of faculty activities in the areas of both scholarly teaching and the scholarship of teaching and learning; serving on promotion and tenure committees that evaluate the quality of faculty work in the areas of scholarly teaching and the scholarship of teaching; offering faculty seminars designed to provide participants with the resources and skills necessary to compose effective course or teaching portfolios consistent with new systems of evaluation in the areas of scholarly teaching and the scholarship of teaching and learning; offering faculty departmental seminars designed to promote the development of scholarly teaching and learning of specialized disciplinary content by covering such topics as the use of classroom assessment techniques, cooperative learning strategies, and problem-based learning; encouraging faculty to present the results of their experiments with teaching in their own disciplines at departmental seminars or disciplinary conferences; and encouraging faculty to conduct SoTL research projects for publication in pedagogical journals in their own disciplinary fields.

References

Boyer, E. L. *Scholarship Reconsidered: Priorities of the Professoriate.* Princeton, N.J.: Carnegie Foundation for the Advancement of Teaching, 1990.

Braxton, J., Luckey, W., and Helland, P. *Institutionalizing a Broader View of Scholarship Through Boyer's Four Domains.* ASHE-ERIC Higher Education Report, vol. 29, no. 2. San Francisco: Jossey-Bass, 2002.

Calder, L., Cutler, W. W., and Kelly, T. M. "History Lessons: Historians and the Scholarship of Teaching and Learning." In M. T. Huber and S. P. Morreale (eds.), *Disciplinary Styles in the Scholarship of Teaching and Learning: Exploring Common Ground.* Washington, D.C.: American Association for Higher Education, 2002.

Cambridge, B. "Transforming Campus Cultures Through the Scholarship of Teaching and Learning." In B. Cambridge (ed.), *Campus Progress: Supporting the Scholarship of Teaching and Learning.* Washington, D.C.: American Association for Higher Education, 2004.

Huber, M. T. *Balancing Acts: The Scholarship of Teaching and Learning in Academic Careers.* Washington, D.C.: American Association for Higher Education, 2004.

Huber, M. T., and Hutchings, P. *The Advancement of Learning: Building the Teaching Commons.* San Francisco: Jossey-Bass, 2005.

Huber, M. T., and Morreale, S. P. "Situating the Scholarship of Teaching and Learning: A Cross-Disciplinary Conversation." In M. T. Huber and S. P. Morreale (eds.), *Disciplinary Styles in the Scholarship of Teaching and Learning: Exploring Common Ground.* Washington, D.C.: American Association for Higher Education, 2002.

Hutchings, P., and Clarke, S. E. "The Scholarship of Teaching and Learning: Contributing to Reform in Graduate Education." In D. Wulff, A. Austin, and Associates (eds.), *Paths to the Professoriate: Strategies for Enriching the Preparation of Future Faculty.* San Francisco: Jossey-Bass, 2004.

Hutchings, P., and Shulman, L. S. "The Scholarship of Teaching: New Elaborations, New Developments." *Change,* 1999, *31*(5), 11–15.

Kreber, C. (ed.). *Scholarship Revisited: Perspectives on the Scholarship of Teaching.* New Directions for Teaching and Learning, no. 86. San Francisco: Jossey-Bass, 2001.

Kreber, C., and Cranton, P. A. "Exploring the Scholarship of Teaching." *Journal of Higher Education,* 2000, *71,* 476–495.

McKinney, K. "The Scholarship of Teaching and Learning: Past Lessons, Current Challenges, and Future Visions." *To Improve the Academy,* 2004, *22,* 3–19.

Munch, R. "Parsonian Theory Today: In Search of a New Synthesis." In A. Giddens and J. H. Turner (eds.), *Social Theory Today*. Stanford, Calif.: Stanford University Press, 1987.

Nelson, C. E. "Doing It: Examples of Several of the Different Genres of the Scholarship of Teaching and Learning." *Journal on Excellence in College Teaching*, 2003, *14*(2/3), 85–94.

Parsons, T., and Platt, G. M. *The American University*. Cambridge, Mass.: Harvard University Press, 1973.

Parsons, T., and Smelser, N. J. *Economy and Society*. New York: Free Press, 1956.

Paulsen, M. B. "The Relation Between Research and the Scholarship of Teaching." In C. Kreber (ed.), *Scholarship Revisited: Perspectives on the Scholarship of Teaching*. New Directions for Teaching and Learning, no. 86. San Francisco: Jossey-Bass, 2001.

Paulsen, M. B. "Evaluating Teaching Performance." In C. Colbeck (ed.), *Evaluating Faculty Performance*. New Directions for Institutional Research, no. 114. San Francisco: Jossey-Bass, 2002.

Paulsen, M. B., and Feldman, K. A. *Taking Teaching Seriously: Meeting the Challenge of Instructional Improvement*. ASHE-ERIC Higher Education Report, no. 2. Washington, D.C.: George Washington University, 1995a.

Paulsen, M. B., and Feldman, K. A. "Toward a Reconceptualization of Scholarship: A Human Action System with Functional Imperatives." *Journal of Higher Education,* 1995b, *66*, 615–640.

Paulsen, M. B., and Feldman, K. A. "The Scholarship of Teaching as an Action System." *Journal on Excellence in College Teaching*, 2003, *14*(2/3), 45–68.

Rice, E. "The New American Scholar: Scholarship and the Purposes of the University." *Metropolitan Universities*, 1991, *1*, 7–18.

Richlin, L. "Scholarly Teaching and the Scholarship of Teaching." In C. Kreber (ed.), *Scholarship Revisited: Perspectives on the Scholarship of Teaching*. New Directions for Teaching and Learning, no. 86. San Francisco: Jossey-Bass, 2001.

Richlin, L., and Cox, M. "Developing Scholarly Teaching and the Scholarship of Teaching and Learning Through Faculty Learning Communities." In M. Cox and L. Richlin (eds.), *Building Faculty Learning Communities*. New Directions for Teaching and Learning, no. 97. San Francisco: Jossey-Bass, 2004.

Robinson, J. M., and Nelson C. E. "Institutionalizing and Diversifying a Vision of the Scholarship of Teaching and Learning." *Journal on Excellence in College Teaching*, *14*(2/3), 2003, 95–118.

Shulman, L. "Knowledge and Teaching: Foundation of the New Reform." *Harvard Educational Review*, 1987, *57*, 1–22.

Shulman, L. S. "Teaching as Community Property: Putting an End to Pedagogical Solitude." *Change*, 1993, *25*(6), 6–7.

Shulman, L. S. "Foreword." In M. T. Huber and S. P. Morreale (eds.), *Disciplinary Styles in the Scholarship of Teaching and Learning: Exploring Common Ground*. Washington, D.C.: American Association for Higher Education, 2002.

Shulman, L. S. "Visions of the Possible: Models for Campus Support of the Scholarship of Teaching and Learning." In W. E. Becker and M. L. Andrews (eds.), *The Scholarship of Teaching and Learning in Higher Education: Contributions of Research Universities*. Bloomington: Indiana University Press, 2004.

Theall, M., and Centra, J. "Assessing the Scholarship of Teaching: Valid Decisions from Valid Evidence." In C. Kreber (ed.), *Scholarship Revisited: Perspectives on the Scholarship of Teaching*. New Directions for Teaching and Learning, no. 86. San Francisco: Jossey-Bass, 2001.

Weimer, M. "Learning More from the Wisdom of Practice." In C. Kreber (Ed.), *Scholarship Revisited: Perspectives on the Scholarship of Teaching*. New Directions for Teaching and Learning, no. 86. San Francisco: Jossey-Bass, 2001.

Weston, C., and McAlpine, L. "Making Explicit the Development Towards the Scholarship of Teaching." In C. Kreber (ed.), *Scholarship Revisited: Perspectives on the Scholarship of Teaching*. New Directions for Teaching and Learning, no. 86. San Francisco: Jossey-Bass, 2001.

MICHAEL B. PAULSEN *is professor of higher education in the Department of Educational Policy and Leadership Studies at the University of Iowa.*

KENNETH A. FELDMAN *is professor of sociology in the Department of Sociology at the State University of New York at Stony Brook.*

NEW DIRECTIONS FOR INSTITUTIONAL RESEARCH • DOI 10.1002/ir

3

Much progress has been made in efforts to conduct, support, value, and use the scholarship of teaching and learning in higher education. Nevertheless, to further enhance student learning, many challenges remain.

Attitudinal and Structural Factors Contributing to Challenges in the Work of the Scholarship of Teaching and Learning

Kathleen McKinney

Despite the tremendous strides made in the scholarship of teaching and learning (SoTL), challenges and opportunities remain. SoTL has not yet reached its full potential in terms of foci, collaborative efforts, developmental progress as a field, and application. My goal is to use this chapter to remind us of the potential still remaining so that we can continue to move forward and enhance student learning.

I offer a sociological lens in examining the factors that contribute to the challenges and opportunities in the field of SoTL. I begin with an overview of the concept of SoTL and the progress of the field thus far, turn to a list of challenges I believe still exist, outline and discuss several attitudinal and structural factors that may contribute to these challenges, and offer some thoughts about the future of the scholarship of teaching and learning with a focus on ways to use SoTL for improvement.

Thanks to K. Patricia Cross, Pat Hutchings, Patricia Jarvis, and Sharon Naylor for their comments on a draft of this chapter.

Background

An almost overwhelming and still growing literature on the conceptualization of the scholarship of teaching and learning exists. Certainly there has been a great deal of conversation about Boyer's original notion of the scholarship of teaching and how more recent understandings differ from that notion, other models of SoTL, and similar topics (see, for example, Braxton, Luckey, and Helland, 2002; Glassick, 2000; Glassick, Huber, and Maeroff, 1997; Healey, 2003; Hutchings and Shulman, 1999; Kreber, 2002a, 2002b, 2003; McKinney, 2004; Paulsen and Feldman, 2003; Rice, 1992; Richlin, 2003; as well as Chapter Two, this volume). A few of the debates in defining SoTL will also be discussed briefly in this chapter.

Despite this growing body of literature, there is not complete consensus on the meaning of SoTL. For example, although Kreber (2002b) found some agreement about a variety of issues related to SoTL, she also found disagreement. Significantly, this disagreement was found using a Delphi study with eleven experts in SoTL who are likely to have some shared experiences and interactions. The social construction of a shared meaning for SoTL is fraught with difficulties. Perhaps that is as it should be, given the variety of social contexts (institutional, disciplinary, and international) in which SoTL exists. Nevertheless, this ambiguity provides challenges to SoTL work.

My own views about the meaning of SoTL bear on the assumptions I hold and arguments I make in this chapter. I define SoTL as systematic reflection and study on teaching and learning made public—a definition chosen by an appropriate body of individuals at my home institution. As do many others, but certainly not all, I make distinctions among good teaching, scholarly teaching, and the scholarship of teaching and learning (McKinney, 2004). Although good teaching has been defined and is measured in several ways (for example, student evaluations, peer observations or review, portfolios), it is that which promotes student learning and other positive student outcomes. Good teaching generally also supports department, college, and institutional missions and objectives.

Scholarly teaching is taking a scholarly approach to teaching and learning, as we would to other areas of knowledge and practice. Scholarly teachers view teaching as a profession and a second discipline; they feel that they must develop expertise in the knowledge base on teaching and learning. Scholarly teachers, for example, reflect on their teaching, use classroom assessment techniques, discuss teaching issues with colleagues, and read and apply the literature on teaching and learning. This conception of scholarly teaching is closely related to what Boyer (1990) labeled the scholarship of teaching. All those who commit to the profession of teaching are ethically obligated to work to be good teachers and to practice scholarly teaching; not all, however, will engage in SoTL.

New Directions for Institutional Research • DOI 10.1002/ir

The scholarship of teaching and learning involves systematic study of teaching and learning and the public sharing and review of such work through live or virtual presentations, performances, or publications. SoTL shares accepted criteria of scholarship in general, such as that it is made public, can be reviewed critically by members of the appropriate community, and can be built on by others to advance the field (Hutchings and Shulman, 1999). Although there are other recent trends (examples are interdisciplinary SoTL, program level SoTL, and K–12 SoTL), SoTL work focuses on teaching and learning at the college level and is primarily classroom and disciplinary based. SoTL also involves application or use. Thus, it overlaps with the scholarships of discovery, integration, and application.

Although my argument is that the field of SoTL contains a number of opportunities and challenges, these exist within the context of the progress that has been made and the successes that have occurred in recent years (Cambridge, 2004; Huber, 2004; Huber and Morreale, 2002; Hutchings, 2004; McKinney, 2004). As many readers are aware, there are numerous national and international SoTL initiatives (the Carnegie Academy for the Scholarship of Teaching and Learning, SoTL Clusters, and Carnegie Scholars, for example), organizations (such as the American Association of Higher Education, although it closed in 2005 due to lack of funding; Carnegie Foundation for the Advancement of Teaching; and International Society for the Scholarship of Teaching and Learning), meetings (including the SoTL Colloquium, IS-SoTL conference, and regional SoTL conferences), publication outlets (among them the *Journal on Excellence in College Teaching, Journal of the Scholarship of Teaching and Learning, MountainRise,* and new discipline-specific pedagogical journals), and new modalities for sharing SoTL work (including Knowledge Media Lab and KEEP Tool Kit). Due in large part to all of these, good work at the campus level to develop, support, and reward SoTL is on the rise. Thus, as I have noted elsewhere (McKinney, 2004), we are literally in the throes of a wonderful social movement in higher education.

Challenges in SoTL Work

Along with this progress, there are a number of critical challenges or opportunities in our SoTL work; I propose seven interrelated categories here for consideration. My beliefs that these challenges exist are based on my own experiences doing SoTL and trying to support SoTL in the day-to-day life of a campus and within a disciplinary society, as well as on relevant literature and conversations with many colleagues at many institutions.

First, as Badley (2003) suggests, there is the challenge to increase the emphasis of this work on learning. Currently SoTL in many disciplines focuses on teachers, teaching strategies, teaching situations, and teaching assignments. For example, looking quickly at the articles and notes published over two recent years in the pedagogical journal of my own field, *Teaching Sociology*, about 75 percent of the articles are about teaching tips or teaching strategies and contain little, if any, empirical data. Of the 25 percent or so with data, about half deal with student reactions, student satisfaction, faculty reflection, and occasionally some specific measure of learning for a particular teaching strategy or assignment; the other half are about learning in the discipline. Teachers and teaching strategies, situations, and assignments are all worthy topics, but we must focus more work explicitly on learning, including both student outcomes and affective and cognitive processes. In addition, this work should reflect not only the teacher's point of view but also the students' point of view (for an example, see McKinney, forthcoming).

Second, we must pay greater attention to the teaching and learning of graduate students. For example, almost all of the more than one hundred Carnegie Scholar projects focus on undergraduates. This focus is obviously a key area for our attention. We cannot afford, however, to assume that we know what is best about teaching graduate students or how they learn in both class and other work (for example, dissertations) with faculty members. We must take the opportunity to do more SoTL work on the learning of graduate students.

Third, although a focus on work at the classroom level is critical, it is time to do more SoTL work at the course, program, and department levels. This would decrease the isolation of those working on SoTL, increase the infusion of SoTL into institutional cultures, create a reciprocal link between SoTL and assessment, and encourage greater involvement of students in SoTL research. Such efforts can also move us further along a path to understanding the bigger picture of learning in a discipline, including pedagogical content knowledge and signature pedagogies (Hutchings and Shulman, 1999; Shulman, forthcoming).

In addition, we are challenged to expand the role of students in SoTL. They are, of course, "involved" as research subjects. For example, in two recent national conference sessions on the student voice in SoTL, the primary focus was on using different research methods to obtain data from students rather than on students as collaborators and co-researchers. We need to bring in the student voice not merely in the role of subject but as co-researchers and interpreters of our data and as individuals equipped to use the results to improve their own learning.

Although the choir of faculty and staff singing SoTL is growing, the spread of involvement in SoTL work to some members of the academy, some disciplines, and some nations is still slow and presents a continuing fifth opportunity. For example, many administrators and faculty members remain almost entirely unaware of the international SoTL movement despite the fact that virtually all of these individuals are involved in some way in teaching and learning. As another example, membership in the International

Society for the Scholarship of Teaching and Learning (IS-SoTL), though admittedly a new organization, is predominantly North American and Western. Although certainly not everyone must conduct SoTL, greater breadth and depth of interest or involvement would potentially strengthen the work and application.

Sixth, we have the opportunity to develop new and stronger forms of collaboration across institutions and across disciplines. Such collaboration is on the rise, thanks to initiatives such as the Carnegie Scholar Program and the SoTL (institutional) Clusters, conferences such as IS-SoTL, cross-disciplinary SoTL journals, and Web-based SoTL forums. At the same time, we need replication of studies and findings to similar disciplines and settings at other institutions, as well as more work in the interdisciplinary "trading zone" (Huber and Morreale, 2002, p. 2). Both of these efforts add to the validity and legitimacy of local SoTL findings.

Finally, one of our greatest challenges is to increase the frequency of and the strategies for using the results of this work to enhance teaching and learning, especially beyond the classroom level. The heart of SoTL is its applied nature and potential to improve teaching and enhance learning. Although Boyer's original conceptualization (1990) offers both a scholarship of teaching and a scholarship of application, we have known all along that the scholarship of teaching and learning includes application. As I will discuss in the final section of this chapter, greater application of SoTL at the classroom, program, department, and institutional levels and in endeavors as diverse as classroom teaching, curricular design, strategic planning, and budget requests is possible and needed for improvement in student learning (McKinney, 2003).

Factors Contributing to the Challenges and Opportunities in SoTL Work

I believe that there are a number of attitudinal (for example, beliefs, norms, stereotypes) and structural (for example, organizational, institutional, historical, and cultural) factors that contribute to these challenges and opportunities in SoTL work. I posit several such factors here for further consideration.

Attitudinal and Belief. First in the list of factors is the lack of consensus about what is meant by SoTL. There are several debates related to meanings of SoTL. For example, there is some debate about the relationship between SoTL and assessment (not assessment as grading or evaluating students, but assessment as gathering and analyzing evidence of student learning and other outcomes for improvement). Hutchings (personal communication, 2005) calls them "cousins." Although I believe there is significant overlap between these two types of work, there are also differences in degree and emphasis. My view of this relationship is summarized in Table 3.1.

Table 3.1. Comparison Between SoTL and Assessment

Characteristic	Assessment	SoTL
Purpose	For internal use for improvement and internal and limited external accountability	For internal use for improvement but also wide public external use in terms of adding to the literature and knowledge base and faculty productivity (presentations and publications)
Audience	Primarily a local audience and not public	By definition, is public, local but especially external and beyond local audience, widely shared
Disciplinary emphasis	Both a discipline and broader (college, institution) nature	Discipline based, though we also have work in the interdisciplinary trading zone of SoTL
Levels	Classroom, course, program, department, college, and institution levels but especially the broader, more macro levels	Primarily classroom, course, program
Role of Institutional Review Board (IRB)	Often not needing IRB approval	Must have IRB approval due to the intent to make public via presentations and/or publications
Methods	Uses many methods but more often than SoTL uses institutional data, large surveys, measures beyond learning (retention, satisfaction, graduation rates)	Uses many methods, often those from the particular discipline
Use of past literature	Less likely than SoTL to draw explicitly on past research	Must use and cite past research
Peer review	Less likely to be peer reviewed	Peer reviewed
Resistance	More resistance from faculty and more acceptance (albeit resigned) from administrators (especially in the past)	More acceptance by faculty and more resistance by administrators
Value, reward	Varies by setting but often insufficient	Varies by setting but often insufficient

What should the relationship between SoTL and assessment be? Perhaps the ideal relationship would vary by institutional mission or discipline, but SoTL and assessment certainly have the potential for reciprocal benefits. That is, on campuses where resistance to assessment is still strong, perhaps SoTL can be a step toward assessment in a way that faculty will appreciate and respect. As SoTL is peer reviewed and made public through traditional ways, faculty may be willing to conduct SoTL work and can then be helped to see that some such work can also be used for assessment purposes. Similarly, faculty members at institutions or in disciplines with a long and strong tradition of classroom and program assessment can be encouraged to obtain Institutional Review Board approval for conducting such work and to present and publish it as SoTL. Both assessment and SoTL should be used by faculty members, individually and as a whole, to improve teaching and learning at the course, program, institutional, and disciplinary levels. These ideas were recently reinforced for me when I attended a stimulating session about possible collaborations among assessment staff, faculty doing SoTL, and university archivists presented at the 2005 Carnegie Academy for the Scholarship of Teaching and Learning Colloquium (Lauer-Glebov and McFarland, 2005).

There are other definitional issues related to the challenges in SoTL. There may be cross-national differences in the meaning of SoTL. In my reading of some of the work by colleagues in other countries and in discussions at professional meetings, I have gleaned that SoTL may sometimes include scholarly teaching, faculty development for teaching, and using one's traditional research in the classroom, in addition to systematic study of teaching and learning made public. For example, interesting articles by colleagues in Canada, Australia, and the United Kingdom offer broader definitions of SoTL than those proposed in the United States (Benjamin, 2000; Kreber, 2003; Lueddeke, 2003). Yet it may be that these differences are actually differences by discipline or institutional type rather than cross-national. Although Kreber's work contained experts from three countries, the Delphi methodology and a panel of eleven were not conducive to drawing conclusions about differences by nation (Kreber, 2001).

I have also noticed similar differences in meaning as I have offered workshops on SoTL at several institutions varying in size, location, and mission and worked with diverse institutions in a SoTL cluster of schools. Although there are certainly exceptions, research extensive and research intensive universities focus on a view of SoTL as published and presented empirical research; other types of schools often include components of scholarly teaching as well and may put less emphasis on publications. Systematic research could confirm or fail to confirm these differences.

Disciplinary differences in the meaning of SoTL tend to be around issues of methodology. As a sociologist, for example, I tend to view SoTL as involving the use of methods such as interviews, questionnaires, or quasi-experiments. In some related disciplines, researchers might use focus groups or content analysis. For a creative writing colleague, reflecting on teaching and publishing a poem about this reflection could be SoTL. Although on the surface, it may appear that those in different disciplines are interested in different SoTL questions or problems, as I consider the topics in disciplinary-based pedagogical journals or in the work of over one hundred Carnegie Scholars, I think there is much more similarity than difference in the general questions posed.

Another definitional issue is the breadth of the concept of scholarship (Braxton, Luckey, and Helland, 2002; Paulsen and Feldman, 1995, 2003). In these debates over meaning, all activities and processes in our academic world (service, teaching, community engagement, administration, and research) have been viewed by some as scholarly and sometimes as scholarship. This very broad view is problematic in a number of ways. First, it could imply that teaching has little value in its own right; it has value only as a form of scholarship. Second, it seems to me that a course could be developed in a manner that is not scholarly (with little reflection, peer consultation, or review of literature) and does not produce a public product for peer critique and review (scholarship). And, finally, what are the implications for faculty evaluation if everything we do is seen as scholarship rather than making differentiations among academic activity, scholarly activity, and scholarship?

On the one hand, these debates about the meaning of SoTL seem both inevitable and functional, allowing inclusiveness, diversity, and fit to disciplinary preferences and institutional context. On the other hand, this ambiguity and lack of consensus can be problematic, resulting in confusion, questions of legitimacy, difficulties in persuading nonbelievers, and concerns about the appropriate mission of new SoTL journals, organizations, or conferences. The question of whether we need a consensus on the meaning of SoTL is not easily resolved. I believe, however, that lack of a consensus contributes to other factors that create or maintain some of the challenges in SoTL work.

Due in part to ambiguity of meaning, we also have a lack of shared beliefs about evaluation standards for SoTL, which contributes to some of the SoTL challenges. Although there is some agreement on the general characteristics of scholarship, including that it must be made public, available for peer review based on accepted standards, and be of a nature that can be replicated and expanded on by other scholars (Glassick, 2000; Shulman, 1999), we have less agreement both between and within disciplines and institutions about the nature of those accepted standards. This is especially the case for SoTL work in the gray areas, that is, work that is seen by some as scholarly teaching and by others as SoTL (for example, a course portfolio shared with colleagues in a department) or work that does not fit quantitative or deductive or experimental paradigms. As I have discussed elsewhere,

> It is critical to maintain high standards in SoTL work. But what does that mean? Do we always apply traditional standards of social science [or education] research such as large N sizes, preferences for quantitative work, settings beyond the local, application of macro level theories, and generalizability based

only on probability samples? What then becomes of classroom research, for example, for those of us doing SoTL but not using quantitative questionnaires with students in mass classes of Introduction to Sociology across the nation [for example]? Can SoTL that uses small Ns, is local, qualitative, and social psychological, for example, offer anything? I think so. I think there is value to readers of a strong and informative literature review, of modeling methodologies that might be replicated by others, of contributing a study that is one piece of the puzzle that forms an important picture in conjunction with other studies in the literature, of offering findings from students in one setting that provoke reflection, experimentation and changes in practice by other instructors in their settings, of helping to support existing theory or results from other literatures, and of confirming what we believe to be "obvious." Must the use of different or additional standards always be interpreted as lower standards [McKinney, 2005, p. 418]?

Other values and norms about scholarship exist and can challenge our SoTL work. Many of these come from the socialization process we receive in graduate school. In the United States, at least, most of us receive this socialization at research extensive institutions where scholarship generally means traditional disciplinary research on disciplinary content, not on teaching or learning. Although these beliefs seem to be moderating somewhat, a common message is that teaching is less important and prestigious than research, and accepting a position at a "teaching school" is of lower status and prestige than accepting a position at a "research school" (Wright and others, 2004). Even when scholarship and research include SoTL, traditional disciplinary work is often privileged over SoTL. I believe this socialization continues to some degree in our faculty positions and through many of our disciplinary associations.

Ambiguity about meaning, lack of consensus on beliefs about evaluation standards, and values and norms acquired through socialization all contribute to stereotypes about SoTL work held by decision makers and faculty colleagues. Stereotypes that I have heard expressed include that SoTL is different from other scholarship, of lower quality, cannot be generalized or used by others, and involves questionable peer review in less traditional outlets such as online journals and portfolios. As with most other stereotypes, there is a kernel of truth to these perceptions of difference, but this kernel of truth is then exaggerated and overgeneralized. One outcome may be a stigma attached to those doing SoTL work when, in fact, many talented and prestigious individuals are excited by and choose to engage in SoTL.

Structural. In interaction with the attitudinal factors contributing to the challenges and opportunities in SoTL work, there are structural factors as well. For instance, there is the history of the development of the SoTL movement. Before the SoTL initiatives at the national level of the past decade or so, the movement started in the disciplines and was limited to a small, often marginalized group within most disciplines and organizations. The SoTL movement involved very slow change and tended to be separate from other disciplinary trends (Huber and Morreale, 2002; McKinney and Howery, forthcoming). I would venture to say that this description still holds to varying degrees in many disciplines today.

Situational constraints of SoTL research also contribute to the challenges we face. For example, ethical issues with human subjects (such as informed consent, right to privacy, and protection from harm), classroom and program situations that bear on the feasibility of the use of certain methodologies (random samples or random assignment, experiments, and large surveys, for example), and insufficient external funding also affect views of the legitimacy, value, and evaluation of SoTL.

Furthermore, those with formal and informal power in the academy have the greatest influence in the social construction of scholarship in general and SoTL more specifically (for example, the definition of SoTL, the value of SoTL, and the rewards for SoTL work). Common bases of power in higher education include position, information, expertise, and coercion. Thus, those with power include administrators, faculty with traditional research status, and those with strong reputations outside their institution, at institutions with large amounts of outside funding, and at research extensive institutions. It has been my experience that some of these individuals hold narrower views of scholarship that do not encompass or at least do not value SoTL work. Because of their power, their definitions of scholarship may dominate.

The relatively lower status of SoTL and SoTL outlets in many disciplines and institutions contributes to inadequate resources and social capital for SoTL work as well as inadequate or misaligned rewards for SoTL (see also Chapters Six and Seven, this volume). Thus, despite institutional missions that emphasize teaching and learning, resources and rewards for traditional scholarship are generally greater than that for SoTL. Individuals may also be concerned about their future careers. For example, in a small study in 2002 of the status of SoTL on one research intensive campus, 94 percent of respondents indicated that the impact on their careers of doing SoTL would be negative (46 percent) or neutral (48 percent) (McKinney and others, 2004).

Given the attitudes, status, and power described above, in combination with conditions in academe such as budget crises and work overload, there is insufficient socialization and training for current faculty and students to do SoTL. Lack of socialization and professional development may contribute to quality issues of SoTL work, limited involvement of a broad range of people in SoTL work, a decreased effort or ability to spread the work to future faculty and, thus, social isolation of some of those who are involved.

There are also broader cultural systems and values that may contribute to the challenges and opportunities in SoTL, including the relatively low value and sometimes negative view, at least in the United States, of the profession of teaching in general and higher education overall. Furthermore, a strong competitive value system dominates in some societies and in the academy itself, which may affect value and reward processes and structures. Finally, there are cross-national differences in federal control, funding, and views of SoTL by government bodies. These latter structural factors, however, are too complex to discuss in any detail here.

Conclusions: The Importance of Application

The ultimate goal of SoTL is to enhance student learning. Thus, applying SoTL work in many ways and at many levels is critical. I believe a stronger focus on explicit use and application of SoTL can help us meet the other challenges and opportunities in this work, including focusing more on learning, moving beyond the classroom level, spreading interest in the work beyond the choir, involving more students, and increasing interdisciplinary, interinstitutional, and international collaborations. These suggestions require us to become social change agents on campuses and in our disciplinary societies.

At the level of our own classrooms and in other work with students, we can explicitly use the existing SoTL work of others to help us in designing or updating courses, revising syllabi, responding to midterm feedback, designing cocurricular activities, sharing insights about learning with our students, and so on. We can engage in SoTL work ourselves and then add to the knowledge base for others. This is probably the most common form of SoTL application today.

SoTL, however, should also be used at the departmental and program levels. We can improve decision making here by helping to establish a procedure whereby all recommendations for pedagogical or curricular reforms in the department have a base in appropriate SoTL literature. Those who sit on department curriculum committees can offer proposals to their colleagues and students that contain explicit reference to relevant SoTL work. Why not establish a teaching circle or brown bag series in the department to discuss current SoTL work in the discipline and how this work might be used in courses and curriculum? We can offer discussions or workshops for our majors and graduate students on what SoTL results tell us about student success in our fields. Those of us who teach courses on teaching the discipline to graduate students should base that course in SoTL literature and include a section on doing and using SoTL in that course. We can encourage and support SoTL theses and dissertations in the disciplines by graduate students who are interested in this area.

To promote deep and widespread SoTL application, this work must be embedded in the broader institutional community and culture. We can use the teaching center, teaching academy, or teaching committee at our institution to assist with resources and opportunities for sharing SoTL work and any best practices that resulted from such work, with our colleagues around campus. Consider suggesting to the committee that is responsible for updating university teaching award selection criteria that they require evidence showing how applicants have applied SoTL work to their teaching and student learning. When reviewing and awarding internal funds and grants for SoTL work, insist that a required part of the proposal be an explicit discussion of potential application. Grant outcome reports required of those receiving internal funding should include a section on how results were or will be applied on campus. Take an active role, perhaps by providing the SoTL research or facilitating a discussion, in using established institutional processes such as strategic planning, program reviews, or formal assessment as times and places to apply relevant SoTL work on campus. Talk with top administrators about having supporting evidence from SoTL work required as part of the budget request process when funds for teaching-learning initiatives are requested. What about an award or competition for the best or exemplary use of SoTL results in a department or college?

Finally, we can take this effort beyond the level of our institutions by becoming involved in the international movement to apply SoTL. Faculty and staff, for example, can organize or present in a SoTL session at professional meetings to increase the visibility and legitimate nature of SoTL in the disciplines and beyond so as to increase the application of SoTL findings. We can include students in such presentations as well. Volunteer to help produce a disciplinary association task force report on best practices in your major that draws explicitly on SoTL work. Join and participate in the many organizations involved in supporting and using SoTL, including IS-SoTL and the Carnegie Foundation, and share with colleagues locally and in disciplinary associations what these organizations are doing and examples of the use of SoTL work.

It is appropriate to end by focusing on recent progress in meeting these challenges and opportunities in SoTL work. Our colleagues around the world are formulating and sharing ideas on new models of SoTL (Benjamin, 2000; Louie, Drevdahl, Purdy, and Stackman, 2003; Paulsen and Feldman, 2003; Robinson and Nelson, 2003), improving such work through the discipline (Atkinson, 2001; Darling, 2003; Healey, 2000), strategies for faculty and future faculty development in SoTL (Cox, 2003; Kreber, 2001; Saylor and Harper, 2003; Thompson, 2003), ways to enhance campus and disciplinary support of SoTL (Cambridge, 2004), strategies to improve evaluation of and value for SoTL (Badley, 2003; Glassick, 2000), and a renewed emphasis on the application of SoTL results (Huber and Hutchings, 2005; McKinney, 2003). I believe the future of the scholarship of teaching and learning is a bright one.

References

Atkinson, M. P. "The Scholarship of Teaching and Learning: Reconceptualizing Scholarship and Transforming the Academy." *Social Forces,* 2001, *79*(4), 1217–1230.

Badley, G. "Improving the Scholarship of Teaching and Learning." *Innovations in Education and Teaching International,* 2003, *40,* 303–309.

Benjamin, J. "The Scholarship of Teaching in Teams: What Does It Look Like in Practice?" *Higher Education Research and Development,* 2000, *19*(2), 191–204.

Boyer, E. *Scholarship Reconsidered: Priorities of the Professoriate.* San Francisco: Jossey-Bass, 1990.

Braxton, J. M., Luckey, W., and Helland, P. *Institutionalizing a Broader View of Scholarship Through Boyer's Four Domains.* ASHE-ERIC Higher Education Report, vol. 29, no. 2. San Francisco: Jossey-Bass, 2002.

Cambridge, B. L. (ed.). *Campus Progress: Supporting the Scholarship of Teaching and Learning.* Washington, D.C.: American Association of Higher Education, 2004.

Cox, M. D. "Fostering the Scholarship of Teaching and Learning Through Faculty Learning Communities." *Journal on Excellence in College Teaching,* 2003, *14*(2/3), 161–198.

Darling, A. L. "Scholarship of Teaching and Learning in Communication: New Connections, New Directions, New Possibilities." *Communication Education,* 2003, *52*(1), 47–49.

Glassick, C. E. "Boyer's Expanded Definitions of Scholarship, the Standards for Assessing Scholarship, and the Elusiveness of the Scholarship of Teaching." *Academic Medicine,* 2000, *75*(9), 877–880.

Glassick, C. E., Huber, M. T., and Maeroff, G. I. *Scholarship Assessed.* San Francisco: Jossey-Bass, 1997.

Healey, M. "Developing the Scholarship of Teaching in Higher Education: A Discipline-Based Approach." *Higher Education Research and Development,* 2000, *19*(2), 169–189.

Healey, M. "The Scholarship of Teaching: Issues Around an Evolving Concept." *Journal on Excellence in College Teaching,* 2003, *14*(2), 5–16.

Huber, M. T. *Balancing Acts: The Scholarship of Teaching and Learning in Academic Careers.* Washington, D.C.: American Association for Higher Education, 2004.

Huber, M. T., and Hutchings, P. *The Advancement of Learning: Building the Teaching Commons.* San Francisco: Jossey-Bass, 2005.

Huber, M. T., and Morreale, S. P. (eds.). *Disciplinary Styles in the Scholarship of Teaching and Learning: Exploring Common Ground.* Washington, D.C.: American Association for Higher Education, 2002.

Hutchings, P. "Movement in the Scholarship of Teaching and Learning." In B. Cambridge (ed.), *Campus Progress: Supporting the Scholarship of Teaching and Learning.* Washington, D.C.: American Association of Higher Education, 2004.

Hutchings, P., and Shulman, L. E. "The Scholarship of Teaching: New Elaborations, New Developments." *Change,* 1999, *31*(5), 10–15.

Kreber, C. "The Scholarship of Teaching and Its Implementation in Faculty Development and Graduate Education." In C. Kreber (ed.), *Scholarship Revisited: Perspectives on the Scholarship of Teaching.* New Directions for Teaching and Learning, no. 86. San Francisco: Jossey-Bass, 2001.

Kreber, C. "Teaching Excellence, Teaching Expertise, and the Scholarship of Teaching." *Innovative Higher Education,* 2002a, *27*(1), 5–23.

Kreber, C. "Controversy and Consensus on the Scholarship of Teaching." *Studies in Higher Education,* 2002b, *27*(2), 151–167.

Kreber, C. "Challenging the Dogma: Towards a More Inclusive View of the Scholarship of Teaching." *Journal on Excellence in College Teaching,* 2003, *14*(2/3), 27–43.

Lauer-Glebov, J., and McFarland, C. "Ends, Means, and Uses: Archives, Assessment, and the Scholarship of Teaching and Learning." Session at the CASTL SoTL Colloquium, Atlanta, Ga., Mar. 2005.

Louie, B. Y., Drevdahl, D. J., Purdy, J. M., and Stackman, R. W. "Advancing the Scholarship of Teaching Through Collaborative Self-Study." *Journal of Higher Education,* 2003, 74(2), 150–171.

Lueddeke, G. R. "Professionalising Teacher Practice in Higher Education: A Study of Disciplinary Variation and Teaching-Scholarship." *Studies in Higher Education,* 2003, 28(2), 213–228.

McKinney, K. "Applying the Scholarship of Teaching and Learning: How Can We Do Better?" *Teaching Professor,* Aug.-Sept. 2003, pp. 1, 5, 8.

McKinney, K. "The Scholarship of Teaching and Learning: Past Lessons, Current Challenges, and Future Visions." *To Improve the Academy,* 2004, 22, 3–19.

McKinney, K. "Response to Hanson's 'The Scholarship of Teaching and Learning—Done by Sociologists: Let's Make That the Sociology of Higher Education.'" *Teaching Sociology,* 2005, 33, 417–419.

McKinney, K. "The Student Voice: Sociology Majors Tell Us About Learning Sociology." *Teaching Sociology,* forthcoming.

McKinney, K., and Howery, C. B. "Teaching and Learning in Sociology." In C. D. Bryant and D. L. Peck (eds.), *The Handbook of Twenty-First Century Sociology.* Thousand Oaks, Calif.: Sage, forthcoming.

McKinney, K., and others. "Using Data to Support and Enhance SoTL." In B. L. Cambridge (ed.), *Campus Progress: Supporting the Scholarship of Teaching and Learning.* Washington, D.C.: American Association of Higher Education, 2004.

Paulsen, M. B., and Feldman, K. A. "Toward a Reconceptualization of Scholarship: A Human Action System with Functional Imperatives." *Journal of Higher Education,* 1995, 66(6), 615–640.

Paulsen, M. B., and Feldman, K. A. "The Scholarship of Teaching as an Action System." *Journal on Excellence in College Teaching,* 2003, 14(2/3), 45–68.

Rice, R. E. "Toward a Broader Conception of Scholarship: The American Context." In T. G. Whitson and R. L. Geiger (eds.), *Research and Higher Education: The United Kingdom and the United States.* Buckingham, England: Society for Research into Higher Education and Open University Press, 1992.

Richlin, L. "Understanding, Promoting, and Operationalizing the Scholarship of Teaching and Learning: A Message from the Editor." *Journal on Excellence in College Teaching,* 2003, 14(2), 1–4.

Robinson, J. M., and Nelson, C. E. "Institutionalizing and Diversifying a Vision of the Scholarship of Teaching and Learning." *Journal on Excellence in College Teaching,* 2003, 14(2/3), 95–118.

Saylor, C., and Harper, V. "The Scholarship of Teaching and Learning: A Faculty Development Project." *Journal on Excellence in College Teaching,* 2003, 14(2/3), 149–160.

Shulman, L. S. "Searching for Signature Pedagogies." *Daedalus,* forthcoming.

Thompson, S. B. "From Two Box Lunches to Buffets: Fulfilling the Promise of the Scholarship of Teaching and Learning." *Journal on Excellence in College Teaching,* 2003, 14(2/3), 119–134.

Wright, M. C., and others. "The Importance of Institutional Context for Teaching and Learning in Higher Education." *Teaching Sociology,* 2004, 32(2), 144–159.

KATHLEEN MCKINNEY *is professor of sociology and Cross Endowed Chair in the Scholarship of Teaching and Learning at Illinois State University.*

NEW DIRECTIONS FOR INSTITUTIONAL RESEARCH • DOI 10.1002/ir

4

This chapter focuses on the role of graduate education in preparing future faculty members for engagement not only in the domain of discovery but also in the scholarships of application, integration, and teaching.

Using Doctoral Education to Prepare Faculty to Work Within Boyer's Four Domains of Scholarship

Ann E. Austin, Melissa McDaniels

Faculty members learn much about the meaning of being a scholar and doing academic scholarship during their doctoral student years. Traditionally, doctoral education has primarily emphasized the discovery and production of new knowledge through research. Over the past fifteen years, institutional leaders, faculty members, and societal stakeholders have increasingly recognized that scholarship can take a variety of forms. Faculty members, for example, have the responsibility to use their scholarly expertise to help students learn, apply their knowledge to societal problems, connect specific disciplinary knowledge with issues and ideas in other fields, and synthesize ideas and present them in forms relevant to diverse audiences. Reflecting the range of scholarly work in which faculty members are involved, Boyer's *Scholarship Reconsidered* (1990) argued that scholarship should be conceptualized more broadly to include synthesis, application, and teaching, as well as the discovery of knowledge through research.

Future faculty members are socialized in graduate school to their roles and the expectations they will face. During the past decade and a half, partly in response to societal interest in the quality of education offered in American universities and colleges, interest in doctoral education and the process through which prospective scholars prepare for their future roles has increased. Situated within a broader literature on the graduate experience, this chapter focuses on doctoral education in relation to Boyer's four

NEW DIRECTIONS FOR INSTITUTIONAL RESEARCH, no. 129, Spring 2006 © Wiley Periodicals, Inc.
Published online in Wiley InterScience (www.interscience.wiley.com) • DOI: 10.1002/ir.171

domains of scholarship. Specifically, this chapter addresses the question of how the doctoral experience can most effectively prepare the next generation of faculty for the array of scholarly responsibilities they will face.

As preface to the discussion of doctoral education, the chapter begins with a brief review of the four kinds of scholarship conceptualized in Boyer's work (and expanded by later thinkers) and an overview of relevant research findings about the extent to which doctoral education currently prepares students to understand and conduct different forms of scholarship. We then turn to the major issue addressed by the chapter: the competencies and appreciations that doctoral students should develop in preparation for fruitful work within and across the four domains. Third, we discuss a conceptual approach to helping doctoral students understand scholarship across the four domains. Finally, the chapter highlights some of the challenges involved in preparing future scholars to work across the four domains of scholarship.

Overview of the Four Domains of Scholarship

The broader definition of scholarship first developed by Boyer and Rice in *Scholarship Reconsidered* (Boyer, 1990) posited four domains: the scholarship of application, the scholarship of discovery, the scholarship of integration, and the scholarship of teaching. Over the past fifteen years, writers have deepened and expanded the definitions of each of these forms of scholarship, as well as explored the implications of the four domains of scholarship for institutional structures and policies (Braxton, Luckey, and Helland, 2002) and for assessment of faculty work (Glassick, Huber, and Maeroff, 1997). In this section, we briefly describe each domain of scholarship and provide a few examples of the implications of each domain for doctoral education.

Scholarship of Application. Also known as the scholarship of engagement (Boyer, 1996) and outreach scholarship (Lerner and Simon, 1998), the scholarship of application involves the use of a scholar's disciplinary knowledge to address important individual, institutional, and societal problems (Boyer, 1990). Doctoral students who hope to engage in this type of work must be able to solve problems of importance to policymakers, community members, corporate leaders, and other stakeholders. In addition, they must have the skills to communicate with these diverse stakeholders, being open to using alternative communication channels and language understandable to those without disciplinary expertise. Doctoral students need to know the criteria for quality work in this domain and understand how to ensure their work is publicly available and evaluated.

Scholarship of Discovery. The scholarship of discovery most closely resembles what is traditionally thought of as research: the creation or discovery of new knowledge. Original research requires qualities such as enthusiasm for the subject matter, creativity, critical thought, perseverance, and attention to detail. Doctoral students need to develop these qualities and gain experience presenting scholarly work in peer-reviewed books, articles in research journals, and presentations at disciplinary conferences (Braxton, Luckey, and Helland, 2002).

Scholarship of Integration. The primary goal of the scholarship of integration is to make new connections within and among disciplines. When disciplinary and interdisciplinary knowledge is synthesized, interpreted, and connected, the work "bring[s] new insight to original research" (Braxton, Luckey, and Helland, 2002, p. 47). This integration is common in many of the humanities and is also needed to address some of the more complex and pressing scientific and societal problems. Some of the products of the scholarship of integration are policy papers, reflective essays, research translations, popular press publications, syntheses of the literature on a topic, and textbooks (Glassick, Huber, and Maeroff, 1997; Braxton, Luckey, and Helland, 2002). Doctoral students need to become aware of this type of scholarship, learn how to undertake the work, and discover the appropriate outlets for communicating this knowledge to the public.

Scholarship of Teaching. Since the introduction of the concept of the scholarship of teaching in *Scholarship Reconsidered* (Boyer, 1990), there has been dialogue in the literature about what it means and how it is done. In their recent work exploring the institutionalization of the four domains of scholarship, Braxton, Luckey, and Helland (2002) asserted that "the purpose of the scholarship of teaching is the development and improvement of pedagogical practices" (p. 106). A few years earlier, Hutchings and Shulman (1999) contributed to the discussion by examining the differences among effective teaching, scholarly teaching, and the scholarship of teaching. They suggested that *effective teaching* results in faculty-student engagement and fosters learning in the classroom. They went on to suggest that effective teachers engage in *scholarly teaching* if they undertake assessment and evaluation to promote improvement in their own teaching practice. Scholarly teaching activity becomes *scholarship of teaching* activity when faculty members make their teaching processes, assessments, and outcomes public, opening them to critique by peers in their disciplines in formats (journals, presentations) within which the work can be accessed and reviewed.

The Four Domains of Scholarly Work: An Integrated Whole. In reality, an individual scholar will engage in each of these scholarships as his or her professional roles, career stages, and research goals change over time. Understanding both the unique characteristics of the four domains and how work in one domain influences, expands, or connects with work in another will ensure that future faculty have a map of the broad territory of scholarly activity and recognize the legitimacy of different kinds of intellectual contributions. Such preparation will help them collaborate effectively with colleagues with different scholarly strengths, appropriately assess the work of colleagues whose work is different from their own (as when they sit on search committees or tenure reviews), and use their own talents in multiple ways.

Research on Doctoral Education

Over the past ten years, researchers have been studying the doctoral experience. Here we highlight three themes in the research on the doctoral student experience that illuminate to some degree what doctoral programs are (and are not) doing to promote student scholarly development across the domains.

Limited Understanding of Faculty Work. Doctoral students typically do not complete their degrees with a comprehensive understanding of what the faculty career entails or an adequate understanding of the history of higher education, the role of higher education in society, and the range of higher education types in which they might work (Austin, 2002; Wulff and Austin, 2004). Doctoral education does emphasize the scholarship of discovery. As students work on research projects in their fields, they usually have opportunities to learn about the questions and issues that drive their disciplines, the methods favored, and the typical approaches for presenting research findings. The scholarship of discovery is usually at the heart of the doctoral experience.

The scholarship of teaching is typically less emphasized (Austin, 2002; Wulff, Austin, Nyquist, and Sprague, 2004; Marincovich, Prostko, and Stout, 1998; Nyquist, Abbott, Wulff, and Sprague, 1991; Nyquist and Wulff, 1992). Students may hold teaching assistantships, but even then, many do not experience professional preparation that is systematically organized to enable them to progressively learn and improve as teachers. Noteworthy developments have emerged in the past decade or so, however. For example, programs such as Preparing Future Faculty (Gaff, Pruitt-Logan, and Weibl, 2000; Pruitt-Logan and Gaff, 2004) and the teaching certificates that have been instituted at a number of institutions now provide structured opportunities for graduate students to develop habits of mind, skills, and abilities as teachers. We suspect, however, that while an increasing emphasis is being placed on opportunities to develop teaching skills that lead to effective as well as scholarly teaching, fewer students learn how to engage in scholarship about teaching and learning.

Opportunities to learn about the scholarship of application and the scholarship of integration are likely to vary across disciplines. In professional fields such as education, engineering, and computer science, doctoral students are probably aware of the ways in which knowledge generation relates closely to knowledge application. Overall, however, research suggests that doctoral students have limited understanding of the meaning of engagement and outreach as part of faculty work (Austin, 2002; Wulff, Austin, Nyquist, and Sprague, 2004). Doctoral students who work on interdisciplinary research teams, study in fields that cross disciplines such as American studies and environmental studies, or work in fields where integration is often a key focus of the work, as in English, may develop some understanding of the scholarship of integration. But we suspect that in the graduate experience of many students, emphasis on disciplinary depth typically precludes exploration of the connections between fields.

Overall, doctoral work usually emphasizes the scholarship of discovery more than scholarship in the other three domains, although specific patterns vary by field. Furthermore, doctoral education historically has provided little opportunity for students to explore the missions of different institutional types and examine the implications of institutional type for engaging in the various forms of scholarship (Braxton, Luckey, and Helland, 2002). In recent years, some professional development programs for graduate students, such as the Preparing Future Faculty Program (Gaff, Pruitt-Logan, and Weibl, 2000; Pruitt-Logan and Gaff, 2004), have been explicitly exposing students to diverse institutional types. Historically, however, doctoral programs have not emphasized opportunities to understand how the various forms of scholarship have played a role in the particular missions and societal contributions of each institutional type. Attention to these issues would enrich graduate preparation.

Mixed Messages. Another theme that emerges in the research on the doctoral experience concerns the mixed messages that doctoral students receive about what is valued in academe (Austin, 2002; Nyquist and others, 1999; Wulff, Austin, Nyquist, and Sprague, 2004). Aspiring scholars notice that although excellence in teaching is often applauded within research universities, the reward structure tends to emphasize research productivity (the scholarship of discovery). Graduate students also report that some advisers urge them to avoid spending time on seminars or workshops pertaining to teaching, since participation in these activities may diminish the available time to spend in the laboratory or on other research activities. In some fields, such as fisheries and wildlife, communication, business, and labor and industrial relations, the scholarship of application or integration is common. In fields that do not emphasize these kinds of scholarship as heavily, the messages conveyed to students about what is valued may not emphasize these domains of scholarship.

Interest in Having an Impact. Research on doctoral education has also highlighted the widespread commitment among aspiring scholars to engage in what some call "meaningful work" (Rice, Sorcinelli, and Austin, 2000). When asked about their goals, prospective faculty speak of their commitment to their disciplines, their eagerness to have an impact on younger scholars and the next generation, their interest in working with diverse people, their love of creative work, and their desire to make a positive contribution to society (Anderson and Swazey, 1998; Austin, 1992, 2002; Rice, Sorcinelli, and Austin, 2000). More than half of the graduate student respondents in the large-scale survey study conducted by Golde and Dore (2001) indicated that they wanted to contribute to the community, but far fewer felt prepared to do so. In other research, doctoral students expressed concern that their preparation was narrowly focused and did not help them consider the range of ways in which they might use their expertise both within academe and in other fields (Nyquist and Woodford, 2000; Nyquist, Woodford, and Rogers, 2004). Doctoral students' interest in using their expertise in a variety of ways suggests their receptivity to understanding and engaging within and across the four domains of scholarship. Currently many doctoral programs may not fully prepare students for scholarship in the four domains, and students may receive mixed messages about the relative value of the different kinds of scholarship. Novice scholars, however, appear receptive to exploring the various kinds of scholarly work through which they can use their expertise and creativity both within and beyond academic environments.

Foundational Competencies and Appreciations Supporting Scholarship in Boyer's Four Domains

Doctoral students should develop appreciations and competencies that enable them to pursue each domain of scholarship, so they will be ready for the array of expectations they may face in their careers. We present five foundational competencies that doctoral students should achieve in preparing for faculty careers in which they will engage in scholarship within and across the four domains.

Understanding the Missions of Higher Education. Understanding the history of higher education, the range of institutional types, and the missions of the various types of universities and colleges in the United States is an important base of knowledge for doctoral students to acquire. Teaching, research, and service have long traditions in American higher education, and the domains of scholarship reflect these historical roots. This knowledge provides the context within which aspiring faculty can see their own work situated. Also, as Braxton, Luckey, and Helland (2002) point out, some domains of scholarship are more prevalent in some institutional types than others. In preparation for faculty careers in the range of institutional types in American higher education (community colleges, comprehensive institutions, liberal arts colleges, and research universities), aspiring faculty will be well served to understand the particular missions of each institutional type and the kinds of scholarly work expected.

Developing a Professional Identity as a Scholar. A key task for graduate students is to develop an identity as a scholar and a member of a discipline. To become motivated and focused faculty members, graduate students must develop self-images as legitimate members of professional scholarly communities who have responsibilities for contributing to the scholarly endeavors of those communities. Part of this development involves learning about the domains of work in which scholars in their areas engage, as well as the skills to conduct work in each of these domains. They also must learn the criteria of excellence associated with each domain of scholarship. For example, against what specific criteria is the scholarship of discovery evaluated, and are there different criteria for the scholarship of application? As part of developing a scholarly identity, doctoral students also must learn to assess their own work and develop habits of seeking advice, feedback, and professional development that enable them to continue to improve their abilities as scholars. Finally, developing a professional identity as a scholar involves finding one's enthusiasm and passion for particular questions and issues that give meaning and purpose to one's work over the course of one's career. Such passion fuels work in each domain and provides some of the glue that connects scholars who are committed to similar issues but work in different domains of scholarship.

Interpersonal Skills. Refined interpersonal skills are becoming even more important for individuals interested in scholarly careers in the twenty-first century. Work in each scholarly domain requires scholars to be able to communicate effectively both orally and in writing to a broad audience, using diverse media. In addition, scholars should cultivate the ability to collaborate and resolve conflicts with colleagues in other disciplines and with diverse personal characteristics (age, gender, race/ethnicity, religion, and others), as well as with individuals outside academe. Excellent work in any domain of scholarship requires the scholar to have excellent command of a number of these and other interpersonal skills.

Ethics and Integrity. Ethical practice and integrity have long been among the more important values of the academy (Pelikan, 1992). Historically, the scholarship of discovery has required doctoral students to learn about disciplinary standards, appropriate treatment of human and animal subjects, and confidentiality issues. Knowing how to work within and across all four domains of scholarship requires even broader attention to ethical issues. Aspiring scholars must learn how to handle conflicts of interest, ownership and property rights, and guidelines for collaboration. Those engaged in the scholarship of application who are working within communities, for example, must develop ethical ways to balance research goals and community needs. Doctoral students undertaking scholarship of teaching work must be able to negotiate the tension between the goal of providing rich, contextual details of classroom contexts while protecting the rights of privacy of student and faculty participants. The quality of scholarship carried out in each domain is closely related to the integrity and ethics of the scholars doing the work.

Intellectual Competencies. Aspiring faculty also must develop what we call "intellectual competencies"—that is, the necessary abilities to engage in the process of conducting scholarly work in each domain. Although specific tasks may vary with each project, the general competencies discussed below are needed to work within each domain of scholarship.

Framing Appropriate Questions. To undertake scholarship that leads to the production of new knowledge requires doctoral students (regardless of discipline) to know their respective fields deeply enough to identify the relevant questions. A student's ability to frame appropriate questions is equally important in the context of Boyer's expanded scholarly domains. For example, students learning to undertake the scholarship of integration need to understand more than the terrain of the knowledge base in their own fields; they also must learn to identify the interesting questions that emerge where their discipline overlaps with and comes up against another field. The ability to frame questions in ways that appropriately guide and bound a scholarly project is a critically important competency for work in any of the domains.

Designing and Implementing the Scholarly Project. Working in any of the scholarly domains requires students to understand the paradigms that underlie the methodological assumptions and practices of their disciplines. They must learn what counts as data in the different domains of scholarship. For example, doctoral students in the sciences accustomed to studying pH levels in soil may be less familiar with the legitimacy of using qualitative data in their scholarly work, but they may need to use qualitative data if they pursue the scholarship of teaching. In addition, students must become proficient in using the tools, techniques, and methods of their discipline, as well as competent in using information resources such as computers and databases. Furthermore, they must understand the relevant criteria for excellence for whatever forms of scholarship they will pursue.

Presenting Results. Doctoral students must learn how to interpret and present results in ways appropriate for the domain of scholarship in which they are working. In order to engage in activity falling into any of the four domains of scholarship, students must make their work "community property [which is] open to critique and evaluation, and in a form that others can build on" (Hutchings and Shulman, 1999). Furthermore, the demand for more applied scholarship suggests that students need to learn how to communicate to stakeholders other than their disciplinary peers within the academy.

Receiving Feedback and Evaluating the Work of Others. Emerging scholars must become familiar with the criteria of excellence associated with each domain of scholarship as it is carried out in their particular fields. They should learn how to evaluate their own work in each domain and how to assume their responsibilities as members of scholarly communities who engage in peer review.

A Conceptual Approach to Preparing Doctoral Students to Work in the Four Domains of Scholarship

Efforts to help doctoral students develop their ability to do scholarship within each of the four domains will have more of an impact if a systematic, conceptual approach is taken. Here we present a framework that takes into account preparation strategies, the scholarly domains within which doctoral students must learn to work, and the stakeholders responsible for providing the preparation. The three-dimensional graphic in Figure 4.1 presents

Figure 4.1. Framework for Doctoral Student Professional Development in the Domains of Scholarship

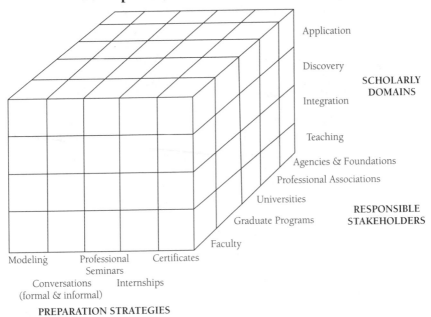

this conceptual approach to scholarly preparation. Faculty and institutional leaders can use this diagram to assess where and how prospective faculty members are learning to conduct scholarship across the four domains. The three-dimensional diagram emphasizes that strategies for doctoral student preparation should be developed with explicit consideration of the domains of scholarship to be addressed and the appropriate stakeholders to be involved in the preparation.

Strategies to Prepare Students to Work in the Various Scholarly Domains. Preparation of doctoral students for scholarly work in the various domains can occur in many ways. Although we discuss five strategies for preparing doctoral students, others may be added to this list. We also note that the preparation strategies discussed may support student development in one or several domains of scholarship. For example, seminars may focus specifically on the scholarship of teaching, or they may provide opportunities for students to learn about the other domains of scholarship and engage in projects pertaining to any of the four domains. Each of the strategies discussed—modeling, conversations, professional seminars, internships, and certificates—can be used in support of any or all of the four domains of scholarship.

The first strategy, *modeling*, involves faculty members' setting examples of how to conduct scholarship within and across the four domains. In research universities, faculty members often work closely with doctoral students in conducting experiments, writing grants, gathering and analyzing data, and writing chapters, articles, and books. As professors model this work and students apprentice, students' understanding of the scholarship of discovery increases. Similarly, faculty can model the other forms of scholarship. A biology professor could involve a doctoral teaching assistant in the scholarship of teaching by conducting together a study of the impact of pedagogical approaches on students' learning. A history professor might involve a student in the scholarship of application through a museum project that provides the public with an interpretation of perspectives on the Civil War. An education professor might coauthor a monograph with a graduate student that involves the scholarship of integration as they write a synthesis of research on a topic about student development.

Informal and formal conversations between faculty and students provide a second strategy for helping doctoral students develop as competent scholars. Advisers and other faculty members often engage students in informal or casual conversations about the work in which each is engaged. Faculty members committed to helping students develop awareness and understanding of the four domains of scholarship could purposefully use such informal conversations to highlight the various kinds of scholarly work in which people in the discipline or field engage. Since observation of faculty is one of the most important ways in which students learn about academic work (Austin, 2002), such conversations are likely to have impact. Advisers also might include specific conversation about a student's development in each domain as part of regular or annual assessments of progress. Furthermore, formal conversations about each of the domains of scholarship and how they relate to each other could be organized at the program or department level (in which examples of work in each domain within the specific field could be discussed) or at the institution level (in which general discussion of what scholarship in each domain entails could be explored).

Third, preparation can occur through *formal professional seminars* for which students receive credit. In many programs, doctoral students already participate in proseminars, research classes, or capstone seminars in which they develop their competencies to engage in the scholarship of discovery. Similar seminars could focus on each or all of the other domains of scholarship. The Center for the Integration of Research, Teaching, and Learning (CIRTL), a five-year project sponsored by the National Science Foundation to improve the preparation of doctoral students in science, technology, engineering, and mathematics fields for teaching as well as research, has developed some model professional development courses (http://cirtl.wceruw.org/index.html). One focuses on college teaching and prepares students to be effective teachers and engage in the scholarship of teaching (called "teaching-as-research" by the project). In another course, participants engage in projects that translate research findings into forms accessible by populations outside the disciplinary specialty.

Fourth, doctoral students might have the option of participating in *internships* in which they engage in one or more of the domains of scholarship. Many doctoral students already work as teaching assistants, but often without opportunities for systematic progression in the nature of their responsibilities, guided reflection on what they are learning, or instruction in how to study (and make public) the teaching and learning process. Explicit attention to engaging in the scholarship of teaching could be incorporated into guided teaching experiences. The Preparing Future Faculty Program (Gaff, Pruitt-Logan, and Weibl, 2000; Pruitt-Logan and Gaff, 2004), which has been implemented at many universities, is one example of a comprehensive program to provide opportunities for doctoral students to learn about faculty roles and teaching at higher education institutions different from the research university. CIRTL has developed internship experiences in which doctoral students in science, engineering, and mathematics engage in internships for purposes of engaging in teaching as research—systematic study of a specific teaching and learning problem, which involves collecting data, developing working hypotheses for addressing the problem, and implementing and studying possible solutions (http://cirtl.wceruw.org/index.html). In addition to internship experiences related to the scholarship of teaching or the scholarship of research, universities might develop internship experiences that focus on other domains of scholarship. Working with faculty members, for example, students might engage in the scholarships of integration and application by developing a report that synthesizes research about an environmental issue specifically for use within elementary school classrooms.

Certificates are another strategy that institutions can use to foster graduate student development within and across the four domains of scholarship. A number of universities already offer teaching certificates through which students complete a variety of activities that contribute to their skills and abilities as college teachers. This concept might be expanded to include requirements that encourage students to conduct research on the teaching and learning processes in the classroom and develop appreciations and competencies needed to work in all four domains of scholarship. A certificate program can also provide the structure to help students track their development across the domains of scholarship as they participate in various activities across the years of their graduate study.

Responsible Stakeholders. In the preceding section, we discussed strategies for preparing doctoral students to engage in work within and across the four domains of scholarship. Responsibility for providing these opportunities should be taken by stakeholders both within and external to the university. We suggest that such stakeholders include the faculty (advisers and faculty members with whom the student interacts), the program or department in which the student is studying, the institution in which the program resides (possibly through the auspices of the graduate school, a teaching center, or a teaching assistant program), scholarly associations, and agencies and foundations.

Using a Conceptual Approach to Graduate Preparation for the Four Domains

Figure 4.1 presents a framework that can be used as a tool for helping readers conceptualize what strategies could be used to prepare doctoral students to work in the four domains of scholarship, which stakeholders might take responsibility for offering these strategies, and what domains of scholarship each strategy might address. By highlighting strategies, responsible stakeholders, and domains of emphasis, the framework can be used as a guide to assess what is currently being done to help doctoral students prepare to work in the four domains and suggest possibilities for expanding doctoral preparation.

Institutional researchers can use the framework to guide studies about the quality of doctoral education at their institutions in regard to preparation for work within each of the domains of scholarship. For example, they might develop instruments to assess the extent to which graduate education at their institutions prepares students with the skills and abilities presented in this chapter as crucial for preparation to work in each of the four domains of scholarship. They might also use the framework provided in Figure 4.1 to conduct an institutional audit, perhaps using surveys, focus groups, and interviews, to determine what strategies or opportunities are currently available to support doctoral student development across the four domains and, conversely, where the gaps are in thorough doctoral student preparation. Such an audit could also investigate which stakeholders are providing various opportunities to doctoral students, which domains of scholarship these opportunities are addressing, and which domains are not addressed through appropriate strategies. The data from such an assessment would help institutional leaders—deans, and department chairs particularly—understand where the gaps or weaknesses exist in the preparation provided to doctoral students for their careers

The framework presented in Figure 4.1 can also be used to help deans and department chairs engage in creative thinking about what possible strategies would be appropriate, which domains might need special emphasis, and where such strategies should be located. For example, the framework suggests that occasions for modeling, as well as any other strategy, might be provided by any of a range of stakeholders and such modeling might focus on any or all of the four domains of scholarship. As a further example, the framework suggests that professional seminars concerning one or more of the domains of scholarship and internships might be offered through a graduate program at the institutional level (possibly through the office of the graduate dean) or through scholarly and professional associations.

While the framework shows conceptually the importance of considering the intersection of strategies, domains, and stakeholders, some strategies are best handled by specific stakeholders. Teaching certificates, for example, are probably best organized at the institution or department level rather than by individual faculty advisers. The framework also suggests that government agencies and foundations are important stakeholders who can make important contributions to improving the preparation of future faculty in the various domains of scholarship. Examples already in place include the Woodrow Wilson Foundation's Responsive PhD Initiative, the Carnegie Foundation's Carnegie Initiative on the Doctorate, and the National Science Foundation's Integrative Graduate Education and Research Traineeship programs.

Conclusion

Ensuring that doctoral students have sufficient opportunity and guidance to learn to work within and across the four domains of scholarship is not without its challenges. Some of these barriers include concerns about possible lengthening of the time to degree, limits of faculty knowledge and ability to guide students in various domains, and long-standing traditions within disciplines about the appropriate focus of graduate study. However, these challenges are not without solutions. Some of the strategies mentioned (such as modeling and informal and formal conversations) can be easily integrated into the day-to-day experiences of doctoral students. Other strategies (such as courses, internships, and teaching certificates) require more time, but this investment in career preparation may be seen as worthwhile by students, faculty, and administrators. Concern about limits of individual faculty members' expertise to prepare students to work in each of the four domains of scholarship can be addressed by drawing on the contributions of the range of stakeholders discussed. The greatest challenge may be long-standing traditions within some disciplines about how doctoral students should spend their time. Strong leadership and thoughtful conversations led by those who understand the importance of preparation for different kinds of scholarship may be the most effective way to address this challenge. Such efforts will ensure the excellence of tomorrow's faculty, preparing them to use their expertise to engage creatively in the scholarships of application, discovery, integration, and teaching.

References

Anderson, M. S., and Swazey, J. P. "Reflections on the Graduate Student Experience: An Overview." In M. S. Anderson and J. P. Swazey (eds.), *The Experience of Being in Graduate School: An Exploration.* New Directions for Higher Education, no. 101. San Francisco: Jossey-Bass, 1998.

Austin, A. E. "Supporting Junior Faculty Through a Teaching Fellows Program." In M. D. Sorcinelli and A. E. Austin (eds.), *Developing New and Junior Faculty.* New Directions for Teaching and Learning, no. 50. San Francisco: Jossey-Bass, 1992.

Austin, A. E. "Preparing the Next Generation of Faculty: Graduate School as Socialization to the Academic Career." *Journal of Higher Education,* 2002, 73(1), 94–122.

Boyer, E. L. *Scholarship Reconsidered: Priorities of the Professoriate.* Princeton, N.J.: Carnegie Foundation for the Advancement of Teaching, 1990.

Boyer, E. L. "The Scholarship of Engagement." *Journal of Public Service and Outreach,* 1996, 1(1), 11–20.

Braxton, J. M., Luckey, W., and Helland, P. *Institutionalizing a Broader View of Scholarship Through Boyer's Four Domains.* ASHE-ERIC Higher Education Report, vol. 29, no. 2. San Francisco: Jossey-Bass, 2002.

Gaff, J., Pruitt-Logan, A., and Weibl, R. *Building the Faculty We Need: Colleges and Universities Working Together.* Washington, D.C.: Association of American Colleges and Universities and Council of Graduate Schools, 2000.

Glassick, C. E., Huber, M. T., and Maeroff, G. I. *Scholarship Assessed: Evaluation of the Professoriate.* San Francisco: Jossey-Bass, 1997.

Golde, C. M., and Dore, T. M. *At Cross Purposes: What the Experiences of Doctoral Students Reveal About Doctoral Education.* Philadelphia: Pew Charitable Trusts, 2001.

Hutchings, P., and Shulman, L. S. "The Scholarship of Teaching: New Elaborations, New Developments." *Change,* 1999, 31(5), 10–15.

Lerner, R. M., and Simon, L.A.K. (eds.). *University-Community Collaborations for the Twenty-First Century: Outreach Scholarship for Youth and Families.* New York: Garland, 1998.

Marincovich, M., Prostko, J., and Stout, F. (eds.). *The Professional Development of Graduate Teaching Assistants.* Bolton, Mass.: Anker, 1998.

Nyquist, J. D., Abbott, R. D., Wulff, D. H., and Sprague, J. (eds.). *Preparing the Professoriate of Tomorrow to Teach: Selected Readings in TA Training.* Dubuque, Iowa: Kendall Hunt, 1991.

Nyquist, J. D., and Woodford, B. *Re-Envisioning the Ph.D.: What Concerns Do We Have?* Seattle: Center for Instructional Development and Research and the University of Washington, 2000.

Nyquist, J. D., Woodford, B. J., and Rogers, D. L. "Re-envisioning the Ph.D." In D. H. Wulff and A. E. Austin (eds.), *Paths to the Professoriate: Strategies for Enriching the Preparation of Future Faculty.* San Francisco: Jossey-Bass, 2004.

Nyquist, J. D., and Wulff, D. H. (eds.). *Preparing Teaching Assistants for Instructional Roles: Supervising TAs in Communication.* Annandale, Va.: Speech Communication Association, 1992.

Nyquist, J. D., and others. "On the Road to Becoming a Professor: The Graduate Student Experience." *Change,* 1999, 31(3), 18–27.

Pelikan, J. J. *The Idea of the University: A Reexamination.* New Haven, Conn.: Yale University Press, 1992.

Pruitt-Logan, A. S., and Gaff, J. G. "Preparing Future Faculty: Changing the Culture of Doctoral Education." In D. H. Wulff and A. E. Austin (eds.), *Paths to the Professoriate:*

Strategies for Enriching the Preparation of Future Faculty. San Francisco: Jossey-Bass, 2004.

Rice, R., Sorcinelli, M. D., and Austin, A. E. *Heeding New Voices: Academic Careers for a New Generation.* Washington, D.C.: American Association for Higher Education, 2000.

Wulff, D. H., and Austin, A. E. (eds.). *Paths to the Professoriate: Strategies for Enriching the Preparation of Future Faculty.* San Francisco: Jossey-Bass, 2004.

Wulff, D. H., Austin, A. E., Nyquist, J. D., and Sprague, J. "The Development of Graduate Students as Teaching Scholars: A Four-Year Longitudinal Study." In D. H. Wulff and A. E. Austin (eds.), *Paths to the Professoriate: Strategies for Enriching the Preparation of Future Faculty.* San Francisco: Jossey-Bass, 2004.

ANN E. AUSTIN *is the Mildred B. Erickson Distinguished Professor of Higher, Adult, and Lifelong Education, Michigan State University.*

MELISSA MCDANIELS *is a doctoral candidate in the Department of Higher, Adult, and Lifelong Education, Michigan State University.*

NEW DIRECTIONS FOR INSTITUTIONAL RESEARCH • DOI 10.1002/ir

5

The authors compare the ideal versus actual academic reward structures at a representative sample of nondoctoral four-year institutions and make recommendations.

Ideal and Actual Value Patterns Toward Domains of Scholarship in Three Types of Colleges and Universities

John M. Braxton, William T. Luckey, Jr., Patricia A. Helland

Incorporation, the most advanced form of institutionalization, occurs when institutional values and norms associated with the object of institutionalization are embedded in the organization's culture (Curry, 1991). Of Boyer's four domains of scholarship, only the scholarship of discovery has attained incorporation-level institutionalization (Braxton, Luckey, and Helland, 2002). In contrast, the scholarships of application, integration, and teaching have not attained this level (Braxton, Luckey, and Helland, 2002).

We have contended elsewhere (2002) that the prevailing academic reward structure poses an obstacle to attaining incorporation-level institutionalization of these three domains of scholarship. In particular, the reward structures of comprehensive colleges and universities and liberal arts colleges are problematic. Such reward structures require some essential elements, which take the form of ideal value patterns needed for such reward structures.

Boyer (1990) advanced prescriptions for the domain of scholarship that different types of colleges and universities should stress in their academic reward structures. His prescriptions align the type of scholarship stressed by an institution with its mission. Thus, incorporation-level institutionalization of Boyer's prescriptions for scholarship domain emphasis depends

NEW DIRECTIONS FOR INSTITUTIONAL RESEARCH, no. 129, Spring 2006 © Wiley Periodicals, Inc.
Published online in Wiley InterScience (www.interscience.wiley.com) • DOI: 10.1002/ir.172

on the value patterns that underlie the academic reward structure of different types of colleges and universities. The patterns of values toward the four domains of scholarship should correspond to Boyer's prescriptions for domain emphasis by the focal type of college or university. This same pattern of values toward the domains of scholarship should also occur at the level of the institution, the academic department, and the individual faculty member.

Boyer (1990) viewed the scholarships of application, integration, and teaching as befitting the mission of comprehensive colleges and universities. Incorporation-level institutionalization of these domains of scholarship dictates that the value patterns toward scholarship that undergird the academic reward of this type of institution should place an equal value on each of these three domains of scholarship by the institution, the academic department, and the individual faculty member.

The scholarships of integration and teaching fit the mission of the liberal arts college (Boyer, 1990). Accordingly, incorporation-level institutionalization of these two domains of scholarship in liberal arts colleges ordains that the pattern of values toward scholarship that underlie the academic reward structures of this type of collegiate institution should place an equal value on these two domains of scholarship by the institution, the academic department, and the individual faculty member.

Moreover, the academic reward structure of comprehensive colleges and universities must entail a lower value being placed on the scholarship of discovery than on the scholarships of application, integration, and teaching by the institution, the academic department, and the individual faculty member. Similarly, the reward structures of liberal arts colleges must also place a lower value on the scholarship of discovery than on the scholarships of integration and teaching. The reward structures of both types of colleges and universities must place a lower value on the scholarship of discovery in order to overcome its perseverance as the most embraced type of scholarship across different types of colleges and universities (Braxton, Luckey, and Helland, 2002). Moreover, in liberal arts colleges, the institution, the academic department, and the individual faculty member must also ascribe a lower value to the scholarship of application as Boyer did not prescribe this domain of scholarship for emphasis in liberal arts colleges.

Methodology

Full-time college and university faculty members holding tenured, tenure track, or non–tenure track academic appointments at the three focal types of colleges and universities—comprehensive colleges and universities I, baccalaureate (liberal arts) colleges I, and baccalaureate (liberal arts) colleges II—and four academic disciplines—biology, chemistry, history, and sociology—constitute the population of inference for this study. A sample of twenty-four hundred faculty members was randomly selected from this population; two hundred individuals from each of the four academic disciplines were selected from each of the three types of colleges and universities.

The Faculty Professional Performance Survey was mailed to this sample in spring 1999. This survey includes items measuring the value placed on the scholarships of application, discovery, integration, and teaching by the individual faculty member, departmental colleagues, and the college or university of appointment.

After an initial mailing and two additional mailings to nonrespondents, 882 faculty members returned a completed survey instrument, for a 36.8 percent rate of response. We conducted t-tests comparing initial respondents to the survey with individuals who responded to subsequent mailings on the measures of value patterns included in this study. These t-tests, which were conducted at the .01 level of statistical significance, indicate that the obtained sample tends to be representative of each population.

For each of the four domains of scholarship, we developed a composite variable measuring the value placed on the focal scholarship by the individual faculty member, departmental colleagues, and the college or university of appointment, for a total of twelve composite measures. Each of these composite variables was calculated using a sum of responses to each item or items that comprise the composite scale divided by the number of items in the scale. These specific items are included in the Faculty Professional Performance Survey. An example of an item measuring the value placed on the scholarship of application reads: "At my institution, scholarship that applies the knowledge and skill of the academic disciplines to practical problems is valued." "I value scholarship that derives meaning from the research of others" plumbs the value placed on the scholarship of integration by the individual faculty member. "Most of my departmental colleagues value scholarship that contributes to the improvement of college teaching" measures the value that departmental colleagues place on the scholarship of teaching. (The specific item or items comprising each scale are available from the first author.) Respondents used a four-point rating scale (1 = strongly disagree, 2 = disagree, 3 = agree, and 4 = strongly agree) to respond to each specific item.

We used institutional type as a basis for organizing the statistical analyses performed to test the formulations regarding the academic reward structures in comprehensive colleges and universities I, baccalaureate (liberal arts) colleges I, and baccalaureate (liberal arts) colleges II. Dependent t-tests were used to test those comparisons that flow from the formulations concerning the essential characteristics of academic reward structures in comprehensive colleges and universities I, baccalaureate (liberal arts) colleges I, and baccalaureate (liberal arts) colleges II. Table 5.1 exhibits the results of the various dependent t-tests conducted for each of the three types of colleges and universities of concern in this study. All dependent *t*-tests were conducted at the .01 level of statistical significance to reduce the probability of committing type I errors due to the large sample size of this study ($N = 882$).

Findings

We organize the findings by institutional type.

Comprehensive Colleges and Universities I. Table 5.1 tends to show that faculty in comprehensive colleges and universities I perceive that their institution places an equal value on engagement in the scholarships of integration and teaching, teaching and application, discovery and application, and discovery and teaching. However, our findings tend to suggest that faculty perceive that their institutions tend to value the scholarship of application (mean = 3.06) a little bit more than the scholarship of integration (mean = 2.94). Academics also tend to believe that their institution values the scholarship of discovery (mean = 3.05) more than the scholarship of integration (mean = 2.94).

Academics in this type of collegiate institution perceive that most of their departmental colleagues equally value the scholarship of teaching in comparison to the scholarships of application and integration. However, such faculty members also tend to believe that most of their departmental colleagues value engagement in the scholarship of application (mean = 3.02) to a slightly greater extent that they do engagement in the scholarship of integration (mean = 2.91). Moreover, individual faculty members also tend to believe that most of their departmental colleagues value discovery (mean = 3.19) more than application (mean = 3.02), integration (mean = 2.91), or teaching (mean = 2.96).

Individual academic professionals in these institutions report that they place an equal value on engagement in the scholarships of application, integration and teaching. In contrast, they also tend to place a higher value on the pursuit of the scholarship of discovery (mean = 3.66) than on the scholarships of application (mean = 3.49) and integration (mean = 3.49), and teaching (mean = 3.49).

Baccalaureate (Liberal Arts) Colleges I. Table 5.1 demonstrates that faculty in baccalaureate (liberal arts) colleges I perceive that their institutions value the scholarship of integration (mean = 3.13) more than the scholarship of teaching (mean = 2.91) and the scholarship of application (mean = 2.99). Although they believe that their institutions equally value teaching and application, they also hold that their institutions place a higher value on the scholarship of discovery (mean = 3.34) than on the scholarship of integration (mean = 3.13) or the scholarship of teaching (mean = 2.91).

Academic professionals in this type of collegiate setting also perceive that most of their departmental colleagues tend to value slightly more the pursuit of the scholarship of integration (mean = 3.02) than the scholarship

Table 5.1. Means and *t*-Test Results

Level	Application	Discovery	Integration	Teaching
Comprehensive colleges and universities I				
Institution	3.06_{AI}	3.05_{DI}	2.94	2.98
Department	3.02_{AI}	3.19_{DAIT}	2.91	2.96
Individual	3.49	3.66_{DAIT}	3.49	3.39
Baccalaureate (liberal arts) colleges I				
Institution	2.99	3.34_{DAIT}	3.13_{IAT}	2.91
Department	2.97	3.45_{DAIT}	3.02_{IT}	2.92
Baccalaureate (liberal arts) colleges II				
Institution	3.03	2.94	2.99	3.16_{TADI}
Department	3.09_{AI}	3.14_{DI}	3.01	3.18_{TAI}
Individual	3.44	3.56_{DAIT}	3.41	3.47

Note: AI = The mean difference between application and integration is statistically significant at the .01 level. DI = The mean difference between discovery and integration is statistically significant at the .01 level. DAIT = The mean differences between discovery and application, integration, and teaching are statistically significant at the .01 level. AT = The mean difference between application and teaching is statistically significant at the .01 level. IAT = The mean differences between integration and application and teaching are statistically significant at the .01 level. IT = The mean difference between integration and teaching is statistically significant at the .01 level. TADI = The mean differences between teaching and application, discovery, and integration are statistically significant at the .01 level. TAI = The mean differences between teaching and application and integration are statistically significant at the .01 level.

of teaching (mean = 2.92). However, they believe that most of their colleagues place a similar value on the scholarship of application in comparison to the scholarships of teaching and integration.

Like their counterparts in comprehensive colleges and universities I, faculty in this type of college believe that most of the faculty in their departments tend to place a higher value on the scholarship of discovery (mean = 3.45) than on the scholarships of integration (mean = 3.02), teaching (mean = 2.92), and application (mean = 2.97).

Individual academics tend to ascribe a somewhat higher value to the scholarship of integration (mean = 3.49) than the scholarship of teaching (mean = 3.29). However, such individual faculty members also equally value integration and application, but tend to place a slightly higher value on the scholarship of application (mean = 3.46) than on the scholarship of teaching (mean = 3.29). They also join their colleagues in comprehensive colleges and universities I in ascribing a higher value to the scholarship of discovery (mean = 3.75) than to the other three forms of scholarship.

Baccalaureate (Liberal Arts) Colleges II. Finally, Table 5.1 reports the findings of the dependent *t*-tests pertinent to baccalaureate (liberal arts) colleges II. Faculty members in this type of liberal arts college perceive that their institutions tend to place a somewhat higher value on engagement in the scholarship of teaching (mean = 3.16) than in the scholarship of integration (mean = 2.99) and the scholarship of application (mean = 3.03). Unlike their academic counterparts in comprehensive colleges and universities I and baccalaureate (liberal arts) colleges I, academics in baccalaureate (liberal arts) colleges II believe that their institutions value the scholarship of teaching (mean = 3.16) somewhat more than the scholarship of discovery (mean = 2.94). Furthermore, faculty members in this collegiate setting hold that their institution places an equal value on the scholarship of integration in comparison to the scholarship of discovery as well as an equal value on the scholarships of discovery and application.

Individual academics in these liberal arts colleges also perceive that most of their departmental colleagues ascribe a higher value to the scholarship of teaching (mean = 3.18) than to the scholarship of integration (mean = 3.01). They gather that most of their departmental colleagues tend to value the scholarship of teaching (mean = 3.18) more than the scholarship of application (mean = 3.09). Nevertheless, they think that most faculty members in their department tend to value a bit more the scholarship of application (mean = 3.09) than the scholarship of integration (mean = 3.01). Like their colleagues in the other two types of colleges and universities, faculty in baccalaureate (liberal arts) colleges II believe that most of their departmental colleagues value engagement in the scholarship of discovery (mean = 3.14) more than the scholarship of integration (mean = 3.01). However, unlike their counterparts in comprehensive colleges and universities I and baccalaureate (liberal arts) colleges I, they perceive that most of their departmental colleagues place an equal value on the pursuit of the scholarship of teaching and on the scholarship of discovery. They also judge that most of their colleagues view the scholarships of application and discovery equally.

Despite the perception that the institution and the department value to some extent the scholarship of teaching more than the scholarship of integration, individual faculty members accord equal value to engagement in the scholarships of teaching and integration. They also equally value the scholarship of application relative to these two domains of scholarship. However, like their colleagues in the other two types of colleges and universities of interest in this chapter, individual faculty members tend to value engagement in the scholarship of discovery (mean = 3.56) a little more than engagement in the scholarships of teaching (3.47) and integration (mean = 3.41) and application (mean = 3.44).

Conclusions

Table 5.2 summarizes the findings of this study. This table compares the ideal value preferences to the findings (actual) regarding the espoused values toward scholarship of the institution, the academic department, and

Table 5.2. Ideal and Actual Relationships Among the Academic Reward Structures of the Three Types of Colleges and Universities

Levels	Ideal Value Relationships	Actual Value Relationships
Comprehensive colleges and universities I		
Institution	A = I = T	A > I, A ~ T
	D < A, I, T	D > I, I ~ T,
		D ~ T, D ~ A
Department	A = I = T	A > I
	D < A, I, T	D > A, I, T
		T ~ A, T ~ I
Individual faculty member	A = I = T	A = I ~ T
	D < A, I, T	D > A, I, T
Baccalaureate (liberal arts) colleges I		
Institution	I = T	I > T, A
	A < I, T	T ~ A
	D < I, T	D > I, T
Department	I = T	I > T
	A < I, T	A ~ I, T
	D < I, T	D > I, T, A
Individual faculty member	I = T	I > T, I ~ A
	A < I, T	A > T
	D < I, T	D > A, I, T
Baccalaureate (liberal arts) colleges II		
Institution	I = T	T > I, T > A
	A < I, T	T > D, I ~ D, D ~ A
	D < I, T	
Department	I = T	T > I, T > A
	A < I, T	A > I, D > I
	D < I, T	T ~ D, A ~ D
Individual faculty member	I = T	I ~ T
	A < I, T	A ~ I, T
	D < I, T	D > A, I, T

Note: A = scholarship of application, D = scholarship of discovery, I = scholarship of integration, and T = scholarship of teaching.

individual faculty members. These comparisons are made for each of the three types of colleges and universities of primary interest in this study.

Although our sample is limited to four academic disciplines and our survey rate of response is somewhat low, the following two conclusions emerge from these comparisons between ideal and actual value patterns toward the domains of scholarship:

1. The academic reward structures of all three types of colleges and universities fail to correspond to the ideal characteristics for reward structures

we put forth in this chapter. Thus, incorporation-level institutionaliza-tion of the scholarships of application, integration, and teaching in com-prehensive colleges and universities and liberal arts colleges remains problematic.

2. We concluded in our earlier work (Braxton, Luckey, and Helland, 2002) that despite the vast amount of attention focused on Boyer's perspective on scholarship, the scholarship of discovery endures as the most legiti-mate and preferred form of scholarship for faculty engagement. Our cur-rent findings reinforce this conclusion: individual faculty members in each of the three types of colleges and universities tend to value engage-ment in the scholarship of discovery to a greater degree than they do with engagement in application, integration, or teaching.

Although our findings lend further support to the enduring preemi-nence of the scholarship of discovery, two findings suggest that scholar-ship directed toward application and teaching may begin to establish equal footing with discovery-oriented scholarship in two of the three types of col-leges and universities included in this study. More specifically, faculty members in comprehensive colleges and universities I perceive that their institution places equal value on teaching and discovery and on discovery and application. In baccalaureate (liberal arts) colleges II, academics believe that their institution values the scholarship of teaching to a greater extent than the scholarship of discovery. They also hold that most of their departmental colleagues ascribe equal value to the scholarships of discov-ery and teaching.

Recommendations for Policy, Practice, and Research

These conclusions give rise to four recommendations for policy and practice:

1. For comprehensive colleges and universities, Boyer (1990) sug-gested that the scholarships of application, integration, and teaching are appropriate to the mission of this type of institution. However, we conclude that the potential for incorporation-level institutionalization of the schol-arship of application exists in this institutional type, and we recommend that the scholarship of application become the primary form of scholarship stressed by these colleges and universities. Put differently, we recommend a revision of Boyer's prescriptions for scholarship domain emphasis for this type of institution.

2. Boyer (1990) prescribed the scholarships of integration and teach-ing in liberal arts colleges. Accordingly, we recommend that baccalaureate (liberal arts) colleges II embrace the scholarship of teaching because of the potential for incorporation-level institutionalization of the scholarship of teaching that exists in this type of higher educational institution.

NEW DIRECTIONS FOR INSTITUTIONAL RESEARCH • DOI 10.1002/ir

3. Baccalaureate (liberal arts) colleges I should concentrate on the scholarship of integration as their primary form of scholarship. Although we failed to conclude that the potential for incorporation-level institution-alization of the scholarship of integration exists, faculty in this type of insti-tution perceive that their institution places a higher value on the scholarship of integration than on the scholarships of application and teaching (see Table 5.1). Such value preferences provide a good starting place for efforts to embrace the scholarship of integration.

4. Changes in the value sets of individual faculty members pose a sig-nificant problem for policy and practice. As previously indicated, our con-figuration of findings indicates that individual faculty members place a higher value on the scholarship of discovery than on other forms of schol-arship. The most fundamental approach to developing a more balanced set of values concerning scholarship centers on the graduate school socializa-tion process. Through this socialization process, future members of the pro-fessoriate obtain the knowledge, skill, norms, and values necessary for professorial role performance (Merton, Reader, and Kendall, 1957). As a consequence, we (2002) have pointed to graduate education as an impedi-ment to achieving incorporation-level institutionalization of forms of schol-arship other than discovery. In Chapter Four, Ann Austin and Melissa McDaniels offer a promising set of strategies for preparing future faculty. We recommend that graduate departments make use of these strategies.

College and university institutional research officers who are engaged in efforts to institutionalize the scholarships of application, integration, and teaching should conduct audits of the values toward different forms of scholarship held by central administrators, academic departments, and indi-vidual faculty members. Such institutional research efforts should consider using our approach and our measures of values to develop such audits. These audits will be most valuable if conducted before changes in policies and practices are implemented so that they can identify possible impedi-ments to the likelihood of success. Then an audit after the implementation of such policies and practices can assess the efficacy of the changes.

Research by O'Meara (2005) concentrates on institutional policies and reforms designed to enlarge the definition of scholarship and accompany-ing ways of assessing such scholarship and the impact of these policy changes. To make such assessments, her research draws a distinction between reform-oriented and traditional institutions. Reform institutions have made policy changes in the academic reward structure during the past ten years, whereas traditional colleges and universities have not made such policy alterations. In our research, we are unable to make these distinctions. The value preferences toward different forms of scholarship held by the institution, the academic department, and individual faculty members might vary substantially between reform and traditional colleges and universities.

Consequently, we urge scholars in the higher education community interested in faculty scholarly role performance in general and in Boyer's perspective in particular to replicate our research and compare the values toward scholarship held by the institution, the academic department, and individual faculty members in reform and traditional comprehensive universities and colleges and liberal arts colleges.

References

Boyer, E. L. *Scholarship Reconsidered: Priorities of the Professoriate.* Princeton, N.J.: Carnegie Foundation for the Advancement of Teaching, 1990.

Braxton, J. M., Luckey, W., and Helland, P. *Institutionalizing a Broader View of Scholarship Through Boyer's Four Domains.* ASHE-ERIC Higher Education Report, vol. 29, no. 2. San Francisco: Jossey-Bass, 2002.

Curry, B. K. "Institutionalization: The Final Phase of the Organizational Change Process." *Administrator's Notebook,* 1991, *35*(1), 1–5.

Merton, R. K., Reader, G. G., and Kendall, P. L. *The Student-Physician.* Cambridge, Mass.: Harvard University Press, 1957.

O' Meara, K. A. "Encouraging Multiple Forms of Scholarship in Faculty Reward Systems: Does It Make a Difference?" *Research in Higher Education,* 2005, *46*, 479–510.

JOHN M. BRAXTON *is professor of education in the Higher Education Leadership and Policy Program of the Department of Leadership, Policy and Organizations, Peabody College of Vanderbilt University.*

WILLIAM T. LUCKEY JR. *is president of Lindsey Wilson College.*

PATRICIA A. HELLAND *is director of residential education at Vanderbilt University.*

6

The author summarizes the findings from a study of 729 chief academic officers who identify both catalysts and barriers to the reform of faculty reward systems.

Encouraging Multiple Forms of Scholarship in Faculty Reward Systems: Have Academic Cultures Really Changed?

KerryAnn O'Meara

The nation's higher education institutions have increasingly become more imitative than distinctive. . . . Campuses increasingly seek to gain status by emulating research centers . . . resulting in many institutions losing a sense of distinctiveness and scholarship's potential remaining strikingly unfulfilled.
—Boyer (1990, p. 54)

Concerned that higher education institutions were losing their distinctiveness in the pursuit of prestige, Ernest Boyer (1990) argued that institutions should return to their roots and reward faculty involvement in the teaching, integration, and application of knowledge as well as in research. He also argued that faculty reward systems should stress the forms of scholarship most closely aligned with their institutional mission (baccalaureate institutions, for example, should stress teaching scholarship). Boyer asserted that if formal changes were made to reward systems to encourage the discovery *and*

Thanks to Jeff Hauger, a doctoral candidate in the Research and Evaluation Methods Program at UMass Amherst, for his work as a research assistant, Gene Rice for his involvement in and support of this research, and John Braxton for his editorial work on this chapter and invitation to share this work here.

NEW DIRECTIONS FOR INSTITUTIONAL RESEARCH, no. 129, Spring 2006 © Wiley Periodicals, Inc.
Published online in Wiley InterScience (www.interscience.wiley.com) • DOI: 10.1002/ir.173

teaching, integration, and application of knowledge, there would be greater acceptance and appreciation of these multiple forms of scholarship by faculty and administrators and greater alignment between faculty rewards and institutional mission. In other words, baccalaureate institutions with primary teaching missions would reward the scholarship of teaching in their promotion decisions and not hold faculty back because they were not engaged in the same type of work as research faculty. Doctoral institutions might acknowledge the scholarship of application in promotion and tenure decisions, and the work of faculty in many master's institutions in developing interdisciplinary programs (the scholarship of integration) would not go unrecognized.

Hundreds of campuses nationwide and abroad have changed their promotion and tenure language and put other structures in place to encourage and reward multiple forms of scholarship since 1990 (Berberet, 2002; Brailow, 2005; Diamond, 1999; Glassick, Huber, and Maeroff, 1997; O'Meara, 1997, 2002; Rice and Sorcinelli, 2002; Zahorski, 2005). Yet very little empirical research has been conducted to see if academic cultures have really changed. This is a growing area of study as scholars and academic leaders try to understand the extent of reform in faculty roles and rewards prompted by *Scholarship Reconsidered* (Berberet, 2002; Braskamp, 2003; Braxton, Luckey, and Holland, 2002; Huber, 2002; O'Meara, 2002). For example, Braxton, Luckey, and Holland (2002) explored faculty professional performance to understand the degree to which faculty in four disciplines had institutionalized the four domains of scholarship in their everyday work. They found that all four domains of scholarship had attained the most basic or structural-level institutionalization, the scholarships of discovery and teaching had attained procedural-level institutionalization (wherein the activity is a regular part of workload), but only the scholarship of discovery achieved incorporation-level institutionalization (faculty values and assumptions support the activity).

I conducted case study research to understand the impact of redefining scholarship in four institutions and found that each of the four campuses that reformed their promotion and tenure policies experienced a slightly more balanced reward system, an increase in faculty involvement in alternative forms of scholarship, and greater faculty satisfaction with their institutional work life. The Carnegie Foundation's 1997 national survey of college and university faculty explored the emphasis put on different forms of scholarship over the previous five years and found that nearly half the faculty at research universities said greater emphasis was being placed on teaching than five years before (Huber, 2002).

Given the hundreds of campuses that reformed their reward systems as Boyer (1990) and others (Diamond, 1993, 1999; Glassick, Huber, and Maeroff, 1997; Lynton, 1995; Rice, 1996) suggested, additional research is needed to explore whether these reforms resulted in the culture change that was predicted. If so, what forces supported the change, and what forces thwarted it?

Framework for This Study

This study was guided by the literature on organizational change and organizational culture in higher education systems (Bergquist, 1992; Bolman and Deal, 1997; Eckel, Green, Hill, and Mallon, 1999; Kezar, 2002; Kuh and Whitt, 1988; Schein, 1992) and on faculty roles and rewards (Blackburn and Lawrence, 1995; Boyer, 1990; Diamond, 1999; Rice, 1996; Rice and Sorcinelli, 2002). In addition, research and literature discussing the important differences across institutional types informed this work (Clark, 1987; Finnegan and Gamson, 1996; Prince, 2000; Ruscio, 1987; Ward and Wolf-Wendel, 2004).

Over the past ten years, many forces have pushed institutions to establish a closer balance among teaching, research, and service in reward systems and to support multiple forms of scholarship (Diamond, 1993, 1999; Lynton, 1995; Rice, 1996; Rice and Sorcinelli, 2002). In addition, many barriers to change have been identified in studies of academic reward systems (Braxton, Luckey, and Holland, 2002; Eckel, Green, Hill, and Mallon, 1999; Kezar, 2002; Rice and Sorcinelli, 2002). For example, research has shown the important role that leaders such as chief academic officers (CAOs), department chairs, and deans play in promotion and tenure systems and in how scholarship is defined, assessed, and rewarded (Eckel, Green, Hill, and Mallon, 1999; Tierney and Bensimon, 1996). An institution's history and culture of valuing or not valuing teaching as a scholarly activity will greatly influence whether a new reform naming teaching as scholarship will be accepted (Huber, 2002). Rice (1996, p. 8) observes that the "assumptive world of the academic professional," which values independent basic research over applied and collaborative work, has a significant influence on faculty roles and rewards in almost all institutional types. External pressures from invisible colleges, parents, or accrediting agencies have been found to be important forces for change (Birnbaum, 1988; Eckel, Green, Hill, and Mallon, 1999). Bolman and Deal (1997) have suggested that human resource, structural, political, and cultural and symbolic forces often thwart change and reform. Thus, research on organizational culture and change in faculty roles and rewards suggests three categories of relevant catalysts in reforming reward systems to encourage multiple forms of scholarship: external pressures, cultural elements, and leadership. Bolman and Deal's four frames—structural, human resource, political, and symbolic—categorize the barriers.

How individuals make meaning of change within academic communities will be influenced by their role (faculty member, department chair, dean), discipline, career stage, and institutional type. While research suggests that some subgroups may be more likely to embrace a broader definition of scholarship than others, real change must penetrate the entire institution (Bergquist, 1992; Eckel, Green, Hill, and Mallon, 1999; Kezar, 2002; Kuh and Whitt, 1988). Accordingly, it is important to understand the pockets of support or resistance among institutional subcultures defined by academic role, discipline, and career stage.

The movement to reward multiple forms of scholarship has meant different things at different types of institutions. Many research universities have reformed their reward system as Boyer suggested to elevate the status of the scholarship of teaching, while many liberal arts colleges have tried to alter a culture focused on teaching and institutional service to one that rewards teaching as a form of scholarship and also encourages discovery and integration (Huber, 2002; O'Meara, 2005a; Zahorski, 2005). Thus, in framing the research and analyzing the data, I considered the starting points of different institutional types with regard to faculty roles and rewards (Braxton, Luckey, and Holland, 2002; Clark, 1987; O'Meara, 2005a; Ward and Wolf-Wendel, 2004).

This study had three guiding research questions:

- What are the catalysts to reform?
- What are the barriers to reform?
- Does making formal policy changes to encourage multiple forms of scholarship increase acceptance of this work by different campus constituents?

Methodology

Chief academic officers play a critical role in ensuring the integrity and fairness of the faculty evaluation process and promoting growth and morale among members of the faculty (Diamond, 1993). Perhaps most important, their position requires them to have a bird's-eye view of their institution, its history, and its existing and future directions in terms of faculty roles and rewards. CAOs must constantly negotiate the strengths and weaknesses of their academic cultures and thus are likely to have a good sense of current values and beliefs regarding scholarship. Because of their pivotal role in setting standards for and assessing faculty work and because of their ability to describe what has happened and is happening in faculty roles and rewards across their campuses, CAOs are the ideal participants for this study.

Survey research was the preferred method of data collection because little research has explored this area and it provided a vehicle to do initial exploratory research and generalize from a sample to the larger population of CAOs at four-year institutions (Fowler, 1993). The survey questions explored CAO perceptions of how their academic cultures affected and were affected by formal policy changes. Survey items were developed directly from the literature review. The methodology placed institutions into two groups: those that did and did not make relevant formal policy changes that encourage multiple forms of scholarship. Such policy changes include expanding the written definition of scholarship in mission statements, planning documents, faculty evaluation policies, flexible workload programs, and incentive grants. These were the most common reforms made and the mostly highly advocated in the review of best practices literature and in campus studies. CAOs at institutions that had made one or more of these formal changes to their reward systems within the past ten years are referred to as reform CAOs, and CAOs at institutions that did not make formal changes over the previous ten years are referred to as traditional CAOs.

Approximately two-thirds of CAOs completed the survey online, responding to an e-mail invitation to complete a Web-based survey, while the remaining one-third completed a paper copy mailed to them. The results reported here are based on the responses of 729 (50 percent) of the CAOs or their designees of the 1,452 nonprofit four-year colleges and universities identified by the 2000 Carnegie Classification system. These survey responses are representative of the national profile of institutions when compared to the 2000 Carnegie Classification of four-year nonprofit institutions. The majority of CAOs, 498 (68 percent), reported that their institutions had made formal changes to their reward system over the past ten years; 231 (32 percent) reported that their institutions had not.

For the purposes of this research, a decision was made to collapse several Carnegie (2000) categories into three major institutional-type categories: research and doctoral institutions, master's institutions, and baccalaureate institutions. These categories represent three different types of potential responses to the Boyer reform for comparison, as the missions of these institutional types are distinct. Clearly there are significant differences between how public and private, selective and nonselective, religiously affiliated, historically black colleges and universities, two-year institutions, and others consider and reward scholarship (Clark, 1987). In addition, prestige makes a significant difference in institutional context and culture (Kuh and Pascarella, 2004). The fact that the data in this study are not further broken down by these categories is not to say these distinctions are not important, just beyond these space considerations. These distinctions are important to study in subsequent research.

The survey data were analyzed using descriptive statistics and multivariate statistics. In most cases, independent samples t-tests were conducted to compare reform and traditional CAOs' answers to survey questions, considering reform CAOs as the reference group. A one-way ANOVA was performed to determine the differences between institutional type and CAOs' answers to the survey questions. Independent chi-square tests were conducted when the dependent variables were categorical variables instead of continuous variables. The chi-square tests were used to determine if there was a significant association between the characteristics of the population. The alpha level was determined to be .05 for all of the analyses calculated.

Findings

The descriptive statistics from survey findings on catalysts and barriers were reported in previous research but not examined by institutional type. All other data are presented here for the first time. (See O'Meara, 2005a, 2005b, for additional description of the methodology, sample, and findings from this survey.)

Degree of Reform and Types of Reform. The survey responses noting "reform" or "traditional" were analyzed across institutional type using descriptive statistics first. The responses are as follows:

Reform: Doctoral/research, 18 percent; master's, 46 percent; baccalaureate, 36 percent

Traditional: Doctoral/research, 21 percent; master's, 35 percent; baccalaureate, 44 percent

A one-way ANOVA on institutional type ($F = 3.20$; $p < .05$) produced significant differences because of the higher percentage of reform master's colleges (46 versus 35 percent traditional) and a much lower percentage of reform baccalaureate colleges (35 versus 44 percent traditional).

Reform CAOs (68 percent of the total sample) were asked which types of reform their institutions had made in the past ten years. They could check any of the four types of reform listed but had to check or not check each item; thus, the number of times each reform was checked by respondents is the underlying metric for results reported in Figure 6.1. When the types of reform are compared across the three institutional types, doctoral/research institutions are significantly more likely than master's and baccalaureate institutions to note their campus had expanded the definition of scholarship written into institutional mission and planning documents and significantly more likely than baccalaureate institutions to note that their campus had used the new definition of scholarship to develop flexible workload policies where faculty could emphasize different forms of scholarship and be evaluated accordingly (see Figure 6.1).

Catalysts to Reform: The Decision to Change Faculty Evaluation Policy. A list of external, cultural and leadership factors was developed from the literature (see Table 6.1), and reform CAOs (68 percent of participants) were asked to rate the extent to which these factors influenced their institutions' decision to reform their reward system to encourage multiple forms of scholarship. Over half of reform CAOs reported that ten of the fifteen factors were a major or minor influence. This suggests that rather than one factor, like the institution's commitment to teaching spurring change, it is the interaction of leadership, mission, and the discussions generated by *Scholarship Reconsidered* that synergistically sparks reform. I reported these data previously (O'Meara, 2005a) but did not explore the

Figure 6.1. Types of Reform by Institutional Classification

Question: *Please check each of the statements that describe a change you made in your institution in the last ten years. Expanded definition of scholarship through:*

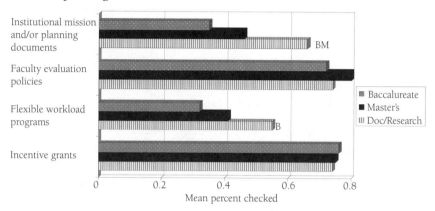

Note: B = This mean is significantly different from baccalaureate colleges (*p* < .05).

differences by institutional type. The following three sections group the catalysts by type of factor and then present significant differences across the three major institutional types (Table 6.1).

External Pressures. Five external pressure factors—encouragement from accreditation agencies; ideas generated by Boyer's *Scholarship Reconsidered;* faculty or administrator involvement in the national movement to redefine faculty roles and rewards; pressures from state legislature, parents, and/or trustees for greater accountability; and partnerships with industry—are significantly more influential for baccalaureate colleges than for master's and doctoral/research universities (depending on the question). These findings are consistent with previous research suggesting the greater vulnerability of baccalaureate institutions to external forces (Clark, 1987). Although there was significant external public pressures on doctoral and research universities in the late 1980s and throughout the 1990s to change their reward systems to be more responsive to undergraduate teaching and outreach demands (Boyer, 1990), it appears that the baccalaureate colleges are the ones that actually responded.

Leadership. Leadership by the institution's president is significantly more influential for baccalaureate colleges regarding the institution's decision to change faculty evaluation policy to encourage and reward multiple forms of scholarship. Also, leadership by the institution's other administrators (besides

Table 6.1. Catalysts for Reform by Institution Type

Question: Please check if, and to what extent, the following catalysts and/or conditions influenced your institution's decision to change faculty evaluation policy to encourage and reward multiple forms of scholarship.

Response scale = major influence (3), minor influence (2), no influence (1), or not applicable (0).

	Doctoral/ Research		Master's		Baccalaureate	
	Mean	*SD*	*Mean*	*SD*	*Mean*	*SD*
Leadership by this institution's president	1.66	.766	1.79	.721	1.94 D	.784
Leadership by this institution's provost	1.29	.458	1.35	.527	1.45	.658
Leadership from other administrators	1.70	.708	1.86	.714	2.13 MD	.772
Leadership by unionized or organized faculty	2.46	.808	2.31	.820	2.57	.709
Grassroots efforts by faculty	2.03	.750	1.91	.680	1.88	.681
General dissatisfaction among faculty	2.32	.646	2.21	.644	2.28	.706
Need to align reward system with mission to meet institutional goals	1.53	.713	1.52	.651	1.67	.764
Institutional commitment to teaching	1.33	.522	1.23	.464	1.18	.460
Institutional commitment to engagement and professional service	1.51	.575	1.60	.673	1.69	.673
Models from other colleges or universities	2.04	.682	2.10	.585	2.18	.625
Ideas generated by discussion of Boyer's *Scholarship Reconsidered*	1.72	.731	1.77	.763	2.02 MD	.785
Pressures from state legislature, parents, and trustees for greater accountability	2.28 BM	.763	2.52	.705	2.78 MD	.477
Partnerships with industry	2.31	.689	2.51	.629	2.62 D	.619
Encouragement from accreditation agencies	2.27	.727	2.21	.744	2.44 M	.690
Faculty or administrator involvement in national movement to redefine faculty roles and rewards (for example, Forum on Faculty Roles and Rewards)	1.97	.753	2.21	.746	2.31 D	.748

Note: M = This mean is significantly different from master's colleges ($p < .05$). D = This mean is significantly different from doctoral/research universities ($p < .05$). BM = This mean is significantly different from baccalaureate and master's colleges ($p < .05$). MD = This mean is significantly different from master's and doctoral/research universities ($p < .05$).

the president and provost) is significantly more influential for baccalaureate colleges regarding the institution's decision to change faculty evaluation policy to encourage and reward multiple forms of scholarship. These findings are consistent with previous research suggesting the greater role of college presidents in internal affairs in smaller liberal arts colleges and the greater external role of presidents in larger doctoral and research universities (Birnbaum, 1992). Likewise, associate provosts and directors of centers for teaching, professional development, honors colleges, and other learning communities (the type of positions likely included in the term *other administrators*) seem to play a larger role in advocating for reward system change in smaller, more collegial institutions.

Cultural Elements. There are no significant differences among institutional types on the cultural factors of general dissatisfaction among faculty, need to align reward system with mission to meet institutional goals, commitment to teaching, and commitment to engagement and professional service. This is curious given that we might expect the more teaching-oriented institutions to note the institutional commitment to teaching as a catalyst and those more service-oriented master's and doctoral institutions to observe a commitment to service as a catalyst. However, ten of the fifteen factors are noted as major or minor influences by all CAOs—and the factors of general dissatisfaction among faculty (which 50 percent of reform CAOs said was a major or minor influence) and need to align reward systems with mission (which 49 percent of reform CAOs said was a major influence) seem to have been similarly important across institutional types (O'Meara, 2005a). Also, the Boyer reform offered an opportunity for every institution to recommit to the value and scholarship of teaching, and 73 percent of reform CAOs noted the institutional commitment to teaching as a major catalyst. Because the movement to redefine scholarship to include application and engagement was smaller than the movement to recognize teaching and because 44 percent of all reform CAOs noted it was a major influence, this catalyst also seems to have been similarly important across institutional types, albeit less than the institutional commitment to teaching factor.

Barriers to Rewarding Multiple Forms of Scholarship. Just as with catalysts, a list of barriers was developed from the literature. Whereas the catalysts grouped effectively into external, leadership, and cultural factors, the barriers were somewhat more internal, structural, political, and human resource related, so we used the four frames developed by Bolman and Deal (1997) for examining organizational problems and change (see Table 6.2). While the categories may appear tidy, each of the barriers has multiple facets. For example, "insufficient training for department chairs" might be categorized here as a human resource barrier, but it also has structural and political implications. Thus, the categorization is presented more as an efficient way to situate the primary concern in the twenty barriers than as a definitive framework in and of itself.

Reform CAOs are significantly more likely than traditional CAOs to report the following external, cultural, or leadership forces as barriers: (1) the political nature of faculty evaluation, (2) excessive paperwork for faculty evaluation, (3) insufficient training for department chairs and deans, (4) faculty concerns about unrealistic expectations that they excel in all areas at the same time, and (5) unevenness in applying new criteria and standards within and across units (O'Meara, 2005a). The following sections group the barriers by type of factor and then present significant differences across the three major institutional types examined (Table 6.2).

Structural. Master's and doctoral universities report higher Carnegie aspirations, higher research expectations, and greater pressure from professional disciplines as barriers. Baccalaureates are significantly less likely than master's and doctoral/research universities to find structural barriers related to documenting multiple forms of scholarship for promoting and tenure, expanding a consistent definition of scholarship across the university, and applying new criteria and standards within and across units. Clearly the institutional size of many of the doctoral and research universities makes institutionalization a much more difficult problem for these institutions than the comparably smaller and more homogeneous baccalaureate colleges where, for example, the reward system is more centralized.

Human Resources. Baccalaureate institutions are significantly less likely than master's and doctoral/research universities to find confusion and ambiguity for faculty about what really counts for promotion and tenure. On the other hand, doctoral/research universities are significantly more likely than baccalaureate colleges to note confusion about the definitions of teaching, research, and service as scholarship, and faculty fear that if the reward system changes, faculty careers, and programs will be less marketable or transferable. Again, these findings are consistent with research on institutional size and on faculty roles and rewards in different institutional types: faculty desire to be marketable within their discipline is more of a concern in doctoral/research universities than baccalaureate institutions that are more teaching oriented (Clark, 1987).

Political. Master's colleges are significantly more likely than baccalaureate institutions to note resistance from faculty unions and rejection of the reform because it was initiated by administration, change in institutional priorities, and the political nature of faculty evaluation as barriers. Many master's colleges are state comprehensives with faculty unions and significant teaching loads alongside institutional ambitions for greater research emphasis.

Symbolic and Cultural. The more research oriented an institution is, the more that values and beliefs about scholarship, disciplinary influence, and the nature of faculty careers are significant barriers in trying to implement Boyer reforms. Doctoral/research universities are significantly more likely than baccalaureate and master's colleges to note desire on the part of

Table 6.2. Barriers to Encouraging Multiple Forms of Scholarship by Institution Type

Question: Please mark if, and to what degree, any of the following issues have acted as barriers to your efforts to encourage multiple forms of scholarship:

Response scale = Not applicable (0), No barrier (1), Minor barrier (2), and Major barrier (3).

	Doctoral/Research		Master's		Baccalaureate	
	Mean	SD	Mean	SD	Mean	SD
Desire on the part of academic leadership for the institution to move up in Carnegie Classification	1.58 BM	.725	1.26	.500	1.23	.485
Ratcheting up of research expectations to improve institutional or department rankings	2.18 BM	.759	1.69	.747	1.57	.669
Stance of disciplinary associations in some fields	1.84	.742	1.67	.695	1.45 MD	.583
Resistance from faculty unions	1.35	.699	1.58 B	.765	1.24	.593
Difficulty in documenting multiple forms of scholarship for promotion and tenure	2.15	.715	1.98	.745	1.80 MD	.716
Greater confusion and ambiguity for faculty about what really counts for promotion and tenure	2.17	.671	2.14	.685	1.94 MD	.672
Confusion about the definitions of teaching, research, and service as scholarship	2.10 B	.718	2.04	.746	1.88	.740
The political nature of faculty evaluation	1.91	.720	1.93 B	.760	1.76	.716
Excessive paperwork for faculty evaluation	1.54	.680	1.70	.673	1.56	.648
Insufficient training for department chairs and deans	1.96	.635	2.11	.706	1.97	.692
Vested interests of some faculty in maintaining the status quo	2.21	.674	2.23	.693	2.08	.767
The research orientation of newly recruited faculty	1.93 BM	.753	1.69	.666	1.65	.694
Faculty fear that if the reward system changes, faculty careers and programs will be less marketable or "transferable" to other institutions	1.89 B	.747	1.73	.683	1.63	.673
Faculty graduate school training and socialization toward traditional definitions of scholarship	2.27 B	.738	2.08	.727	1.99	.725
Faculty concerns about unrealistic expectations that faculty excel in all areas at the same time	2.10	.640	2.17	.661	2.15	.682
Difficulty in expanding a consistent definition of scholarship across the university	2.24	.658	2.18	.711	1.92 MD	.709
Unevenness in application of new criteria and standards within units and across units	2.16	.695	2.05	.708	1.83 MD	.743
Rejection of the reform or change because it was initiated by administration	1.64	.723	1.76 B	.725	1.50	.673
Turnover of key advocates or change in institutional leadership	1.54	.664	1.53	.662	1.49	.648
Change in institutional priorities	1.53	.625	1.64 B	.693	1.45	.644

Note: B = This mean is significantly different from baccalaureate colleges ($p < .05$). BM = This mean is significantly different from baccalaureate and master's colleges ($p < .05$). MD = This mean is significantly different from master's and doctoral/research universities ($p < .05$).

academic leadership to move up in Carnegie classification, ratcheting up of research expectations to improve institutional or departmental rankings, and the research orientation of newly recruited faculty as barriers, and significantly more likely than baccalaureate institutions to find faculty graduate school training and socialization toward traditional definitions of scholarship as a barrier. The less research-oriented baccalaureates face less resistance in redefining scholarship.

Acceptance Within Academic Cultures. All CAOs were asked whether it was commonly believed on their campus that aspects of college teaching, engagement, integrative and interdisciplinary activity, and participatory action research could be defined as scholarship. All CAOs were also asked whether over the past decade they believed their faculty had developed a more complex, nuanced view of scholarship. In every case, independent samples t-tests showed that reform CAOs are significantly more likely than traditional CAOs to note these statements as true (see Table 6.3). There are some significant differences when the responses are compared by institutional type. Doctoral/research universities are significantly less likely than baccalaureate and master's colleges to agree that aspects of college teaching, engagement and professional activity, participatory action research, and other forms of newer research might be defined as scholarship on their campuses (Table 6.3).

All CAOs were also asked to rate the level of support for an expanded definition of scholarship among groups by discipline, career stage, and administrative role during the past five years (Figure 6.2). In every case, reform CAOs are significantly more likely than traditional CAOs to rate the constituency (whether social science faculty, midcareer faculty, or dean) as supportive or very supportive.

Discussion and Implications

The findings presented here suggest at least two implications for our understanding of the impact of Boyer's (1990) reforms on academic cultures and reward systems.

First, institutional type, culture, and constraints on faculty work should be considered when initiating these reforms in academic reward systems. The particular circumstances of each institutional type play a large role in why the institution decided to initiate reform to its reward system and the special barriers it found to implementing the reforms. Baccalaureates are more likely to be influenced by internal leadership (for example, the president and provost) and from external pressures (for example, accreditation, industry partnerships) than the other two types. Master's colleges are very likely to have made reforms but faced resistance from unions likely afraid of adding responsibilities to already full faculty plates by encouraging multiple forms of scholarship. The need to compete in the research prestige

Table 6.3. Acceptance Within Academic Cultures: Comparison by Reform Versus Traditional and by Institution Type

	Reform	Traditional		Baccalaureate		Master's		Doctoral/ Research	
	Mean	Mean	t	Mean	SD	Mean	SD	Mean	SD
At my institution, it is commonly believed that many aspects of college teaching may be defined as scholarship.	3.01	2.54	7.63***	2.93	.780	2.91	.721	2.62 BM	.808
At my institution, it is commonly believed that many aspects of engagement/professional service may be defined as scholarship.	2.90	2.39	8.76***	2.79	.734	2.78	.694	2.54 BM	.773
At my institution, it is commonly believed that integrating and synthesizing existing bodies of knowledge into interdisciplinary contexts may be defined as scholarship.	3.15	2.96	3.78***	3.11	.626	3.12	.568	2.97	.591
At my institution, participatory action research and other, newer forms of research are considered scholarship.	3.10	2.72	6.71***	3.00	.635	3.04	.629	2.78 BM	.759
Over the last ten years faculty have developed a more complex, nuanced view of scholarship.	3.14	2.64	9.32***	2.96	.650	3.00	.698	3.02	.675

Note: t-test results compare reform and traditional CAO responses to the question, "Please indicate your level of agreement or disagreement with each statement."
Response scale: 1 = strongly disagree, 2 = disagree, 3 = agree, 4 = strongly agree.

BM = This mean is significantly different from baccalaureate and master's colleges ($p < .05$).

*** $p < 0.001$.

Figure 6.2. Results of *t*-Test Comparing Reform and Traditional CAO Responses to the Question: "How would you rate the level of support for an expanded definition of scholarship among the following groups during the past five years?"

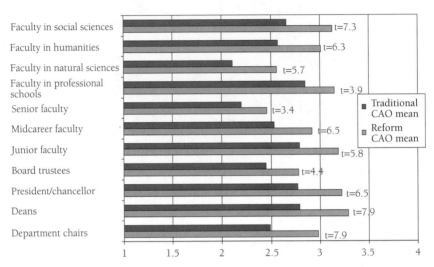

Note: Response scale: 1 = opposed, 2 = neutral, 3 = supportive, 4 = very supportive. All *t*-tests are statistically significant (*p* < 0.001).

game, with its constant stress of recruiting faculty researchers and publishing demands, is more of a concern for the doctoral/research universities than the others. Moreover, doctoral institutions had problems ensuring a common definition of scholarship and standards that are well understood and enforced across disciplines. For baccalaureates (likely smaller institutions), implementation across disciplines, research orientation of faculty, and mission drift are less barriers to encouraging multiple forms of scholarship than the likely stress of teaching and advising load.

We know from previous work on faculty work life that master's institutions, the majority being public state colleges, struggle with frequent shifts in priorities and leadership, and many faculty unions take on a defensive stance to any reforms initiated by the administration (Arnold, 2000). In a similar vein, master's colleges in this study found the political nature of the promotion and tenure process, union resistance, and changes in priorities to be significant barriers. Yet it is interesting to note that there is a higher percentage of master's' colleges than other types that have implemented the Boyer reform. This goes against the perception that the Boyer framework is mostly used by campuses at either end of the Carnegie classification. Although a majority of all campuses initiated the reforms studied here, these reforms seem to have been particularly picked up by the institutions in the middle of the Carnegie classification: those with significant but not the highest teaching loads, likely aspiring to more and greater scholarship, and with a firm commitment to their teaching and service missions.

These findings suggest that some catalysts and barriers are the same within each type but differ across institutional types. For example, the Boyer reforms were always intended to help research and doctoral institutions create a vehicle for valuing teaching and research more (Boyer, 1990; Glassick, Huber, and Maeroff, 1997; Huber, 2002); thus, it is not surprising that values prioritizing research still remain and act as a barrier within these institutions. The Boyer reform is one lever for change but not a panacea for this problem. Until graduate education and disciplinary associations emphasize newer forms of scholarship as legitimate and scholarly, these problems will remain. At baccalaureates, the reform was intended to encourage more faculty involvement in any form of scholarship, including inquiry into teaching and learning, application, and integration despite very heavy teaching and advising responsibilities (Brailow, 2005; Braskamp, 2003; Berberet, 2002). The Boyer reform is one way to encourage this work, perhaps with other supports like release time, course reduction, and professional development.

Thus, the goal for provosts, deans, and department chairs implementing reforms to encourage multiple forms of scholarship should be to identify the key stresses and barriers to productive faculty work overall and to initiate the Boyer reform in ways that help to address them. For example, if it becomes next to impossible to ensure that a consistent definition of scholarship is used across a large doctoral institution, why not let each department develop its own disciplinary definition of each of the four forms of scholarship and methods for evaluation? This strategy met significant success at South Dakota State University (Peterson and Kayongo-Male, 2005). If reforms initiated by the administration are suspect, they might be allowed to percolate first within the faculty senate or union, which should have the ability to shape them, as was the case at St. Norbert College and Franklin College (Brailow, 2005; Zahorski, 2005).

Second, across all institutional types, reforming faculty reward systems to encourage multiple forms of scholarship positively influenced acceptance of this work within academic cultures. The findings also suggest that campus constituencies at reform institutions are more supportive of the broader view of scholarship. While it is not clear whether this greater acceptance existed before the reform or was a product of its campuswide implementation and results, at minimum it seems reasonable to assume that making the reforms will create greater visibility for and discussion around multiple forms of scholarship and that these efforts may result in greater support for the idea of multiple forms of scholarship across campus. The fact that reform campus CAOs were more likely to observe that over the past ten years their campus had developed a more nuanced definition of scholarship suggests a healthy conversation had occurred, one that can only benefit those involved in both traditional and alternative forms of scholarship.

The findings from this study also suggest important areas for future research for institutional researchers and nationwide studies of reward system change.

Areas for Institutional Research. It is important for individual campuses and their institutional researchers to study whether Boyer's reforms have changed academic cultures from the perspective of individual faculty careers. Huber's work (2004) examining pathfinders, or faculty who have pursued the scholarship of teaching, provides such an example. From a micro, or individual, career perspective, have faculty involved in the scholarship of application or integration found career progression and promotion any easier? Have departments made any strides in honoring multiple talents and appreciating different scholarly contributions such that individual faculty feel a difference in how their work is considered and valued? How does this differ by discipline? Finally, do campuses that make these reforms encourage faculty with plateaued careers into new directions? Campus and department case studies, individual faculty portraits, ethnography, and interviews are all methods well suited to these questions.

More than fifteen years after Boyer's reforms were proposed, it is also important for institutional researchers to study their own campuses' second-generation issues in institutionalizing a broader definition of scholarship, as was done at Portland State University (Rueter and Bauer, 2005), a campus well known for having made these reforms in the mid-1990s. What happens when new faculty with research orientations come to these institutions with a broader definition of scholarship? Do they change, or do they change the definition, or somewhere in the middle? Annual faculty surveys noting changes in faculty views of scholarship, records of changes in hiring, and annual profiles of the scholarship of recently tenured faculty might help to illuminate whether the campus continues to embrace or is moving closer toward a broader definition of scholarship in faculty roles and rewards.

Areas for Nationwide Study of Academic Reward System Change. On a macrolevel, it is important for institutional researchers, higher education faculty who study academic culture and reward systems, and researchers at higher education associations and think tanks to collaborate on nationwide studies. For example, studies need to be done across state systems of higher education and within specific institutional types to discover whether changes in reward systems have significant effects outside faculty work life and satisfaction. For example, on research and doctoral campuses that have made major strides in encouraging the scholarship of teaching, do students see any difference in terms of the quality of their classes, their own learning, or development? In other words, does more time spent on the scholarship of teaching (which may have been shifted in part because of a reformed reward system) result in more learning for students? Have the surrounding communities found faculty more immersed in community problems, and has this greater commitment resulted in desired outcomes?

Across campuses, we need to examine which campuses virtually adopted the reforms (Birnbaum, 2000) versus which ones seem to be making promotion and tenure decisions and resource allocations with a broader definition of scholarship in mind. Scholars of organizational change in higher education need to understand better why campuses went in these different directions. Finally, how has the phenomenon of "striving colleges," and academic ratcheting, wherein colleges compete for *U.S. News and World Report* rankings (O'Meara and Bloomgarden, 2005), influenced the implementation of a broader definition of scholarship in different sectors of higher education (for example, liberal arts colleges versus research universities), especially since 2001, as the marketplace has become more competitive? These are questions ripe for exploration that would benefit from collaboration between institutional researchers with campus-specific data and higher education research centers that conduct national trend studies on faculty and changes in faculty employment.

Conclusion

Encouraging multiple forms of scholarship in reward systems is not a panacea for all of the problems that we know exist within reward systems, such as the political nature of decisions, ambiguous standards, and sparse funding for merit. Also, the reforms discussed in this chapter will have different purposes and results across institutional types. However, according to the CAOs in this study, changing promotion and tenure language and institutional mission statements and providing flexible workload programs and incentive grants to encourage multiple forms of scholarship make a positive difference in beliefs about and acceptance of multiple forms of scholarship. Encouraging such multiple forms of scholarship has the potential for effecting change when implemented with a sensitivity to institutional cultures and constraints on faculty time. Further research is needed to explore the depth of change and the challenges and benefits to implementing these reforms in different institutional types.

References

Arnold, G. B. *The Politics of Faculty Unionization: The Experience of Three New England Universities.* Westport, Conn.: Bergin and Garvey, 2000.

Berberet, J. "The New Academic Compact." In L. A. McMillin and J. Berberet (eds.), *The New Academic Compact: Revisioning the Relationship Between Faculty and Their Institutions.* Bolton, Mass.: Anker, 2002.

Bergquist, W. H. *Four Cultures of the Academy.* San Francisco: Jossey-Bass, 1992.

Birnbaum, R. *How Colleges Work.* San Francisco: Jossey-Bass, 1988.

Birnbaum, R. *How Academic Leadership Works.* San Francisco: Jossey-Bass, 1992.

Birnbaum, R. *Management Fads in Higher Education.* San Francisco: Jossey-Bass, 2000.

Blackburn, R. T., and Lawrence, J. H. *Faculty at Work: Motivation, Expectation, Satisfaction.* Baltimore: Johns Hopkins University Press, 1995.

Bolman, L. G., and Deal, T. E. *Reframing Organizations: Artistry, Choice and Leadership.* (2nd ed.) San Francisco: Jossey-Bass, 1997.

Boyer, E. *Scholarship Reconsidered.* Princeton, N.J.: Carnegie Foundation for the Advancement of Teaching, 1990.

Brailow, D. "A Question of Mission: Redefining Scholarship at Franklin College." In K. O'Meara and R. Eugene Rice (eds.), *Faculty Priorities Reconsidered.* San Francisco: Jossey-Bass, 2005.

Braskamp, L. *Fostering Student Development Through Faculty Development: A National Survey of Chief Academic officers at Church-Related Colleges.* Chicago: Loyola University, 2003.

Braxton, J., Luckey, W., and Holland, P. *Institutionalizing a Broader View of Scholarship Through Boyer's Four Domains.* San Francisco: Jossey-Bass, 2002.

Clark, B. R. *The Academic Life: Small Worlds, Different Worlds.* Princeton, N.J.: Carnegie Foundation for the Advancement of Teaching, 1987.

Diamond, R. M. "Instituting Change in Faculty Reward Systems." In R. M. Diamond and B. E. Adam (eds.), *Recognizing Faculty Work: Reward Systems for the Year 2000.* New Directions for Higher Education, no. 81. San Francisco: Jossey-Bass, 1993.

Diamond, R. M. *Aligning Faculty Rewards with Institutional Mission: Statements, Policies, and Guidelines.* Bolton, Mass.: Anker, 1999.

Eckel, P., Green, M., Hill, B., and Mallon, W. *On Change III: Taking Charge of Change: A Primer for Colleges and Universities.* Washington, D.C.: American Council on Education, 1999.

Finnegan, D. E., and Gamson, Z. F. "Disciplinary Adaptations to Research Culture in Comprehensive Institutions." *Review of Higher Education,* 1996, *19*(2), 141–177.

Fowler, F. *Survey Research Methods.* (2nd ed.) Thousand Oaks, Calif.: Sage, 1993.

Glassick, C. E., Huber, M. T., and Maeroff, G. I. *Scholarship Assessed: Evaluation of the Professoriate.* San Francisco: Jossey-Bass, 1997.

Huber, M. "Faculty Evaluation and the Development of Academic Careers." In C. Colbeck (ed.), *Evaluating Faculty Performance.* San Francisco: Jossey-Bass, 2002.

Huber, M. T. *Balancing Acts: The Scholarship of Teaching and Learning in Academic Careers.* Washington, D.C.: American Association of Higher Education and the Carnegie Foundation for the Advancement for Teaching, 2004.

Kezar, A. J. *Understanding and Facilitating Organizational Change in the Twenty-First Century: Recent Research and Conceptualizations.* ASHE-ERIC Higher Education Report, vol. 28, no. 4. San Francisco: Jossey-Bass, 2002.

Kuh, G. D., and Pascarella, E. T. "What Does Institutional Selectivity Tell Us About Educational Quality?" *Change,* Sept.–Oct. 2004, pp. 53–58.

Kuh, G. D., and Whitt, E. J. *The Invisible Tapestry: Culture in American Colleges and Universities.* ASHE-ERIC Higher Education Report, vol. 1. San Francisco: Jossey-Bass, 1988.

Lynton, E. *Making the Case for Professional Service.* Washington, D.C.: American Association for Higher Education, 1995.

O'Meara, K. "Rewarding Faculty Professional Service." Working paper 19, New England Resource Center for Higher Education, 1997.

O'Meara, K. A. "Uncovering the Values in Faculty Evaluation of Service as Scholarship." *Review of Higher Education,* 2002, *26*, 57–80.

O'Meara, K. A. *Effects of Encouraging Multiple Forms of Scholarship Nationwide and Across Institutional Types.* In K. O'Meara and R. Eugene Rice (eds.), *Faculty Priorities Reconsidered.* San Francisco: Jossey-Bass, 2005a.

O'Meara, K. "Encouraging Multiple Forms of Scholarship in Faculty Reward Systems: Does It Make a Difference?" *Research in Higher Education,* 2005b, *46*(5), 479–510.

O'Meara, K., and Bloomgarden, A. "Exploring the Nature and Impact of Striving." Unpublished manuscript, University of Massachusetts, 2005.

Peterson, C., and Kayongo-Male, D. "Ensuring Equity Across the Missions of a Land Grant University: South Dakota State University." In K. O'Meara and R. Eugene Rice (eds.), *Faculty Priorities Reconsidered.* San Francisco: Jossey-Bass, 2005.

Prince, G. S. Jr. "A Liberal Arts College Perspective." In T. Ehrlich (ed.), *Civic Responsibility and Higher Education.* Phoenix, Ariz.: Oryx Press, 2000.

Rice, R. E. *Making a Place for the New American Scholar.* Washington, D.C.: American Association for Higher Education, 1996.

Rice, R. E., and Sorcinelli, M. "Can the Tenure Process Be Improved?" In R. Chait (ed.), *The Questions of Tenure.* Cambridge, Mass.: Harvard University Press, 2002.

Rueter, J., and Bauer, T. "Identifying and Managing University Assets: A Campus Study of Portland State University." In K. A. O'Meara and R. E. Rice (eds.), *Faculty Priorities Reconsidered.* San Francisco: Jossey-Bass, 2005.

Ruscio, K. P. "The Distinctive Scholarship of the Selective Liberal Arts College." *Journal of Higher Education,* 1987, *58*(2), 205–222.

Schein, E. H. *Organizational Culture and Leadership.* (2nd ed.) San Francisco: Jossey-Bass, 1992.

Tierney, W. G., and Bensimon, E. M. *Promotion and Tenure: Community and Socialization in Academe.* Albany: State University of New York Press, 1996.

Ward, K., and Wolf-Wendel, L. "Academic Life and Motherhood: Variations by Institutional Type." Paper presented at the Annual Conference of the Association for the Study of Higher Education, Portland, Ore., 2004.

Zahorski, K. "Redefining Scholarship: A Small Liberal Arts College's Journey." In K. O'Meara and R. E. Rice (eds.), *Faculty Priorities Reconsidered.* San Francisco: Jossey-Bass, 2005.

KERRYANN O'MEARA is assistant professor of higher education and program coordinator at the University of Massachusetts Amherst.

7

The author applies strategic response theory to develop hypotheses about the type of response that public colleges and universities will exhibit as a consequence of state policies to encourage the scholarship of teaching, discovery, and application.

State Accountability Policies and Boyer's Domains of Scholarship: Conflict or Collaboration?

William R. Doyle

Higher education has come under increasing pressure in the past two decades to produce systematic evidence of its outcomes. Many leaders, particularly elected officials, have asked higher education to produce evidence of student learning at the collegiate level. Others want to increase the research productivity of higher education. Still other policies have been aimed at increasing the connection between higher education and industry. Although the links are rarely made explicitly, many of the state policies that have been put into place are intended to encourage faculty work in several of the functions of academic life that Boyer defined in *Scholarship Reconsidered* (1990). In particular, these policies above should be interpreted as encouraging the following forms of scholarship:

- Student outcomes assessment: The scholarship of teaching
- Business and industry cooperation: The scholarship of application
- Research productivity: The scholarship of discovery

Pressure from state policymakers to demonstrate the effectiveness of institutions of higher education will most likely only increase in the future. Quite a lot rides on how higher education has responded and will respond

NEW DIRECTIONS FOR INSTITUTIONAL RESEARCH, no. 129, Spring 2006   © Wiley Periodicals, Inc.
Published online in Wiley InterScience (www.interscience.wiley.com) • DOI: 10.1002/ir.174

to the challenge of providing outcomes information on scholarship in these different domains.

Understanding the circumstances under which institutions are more or less likely to respond to external calls for assessment of outcomes is an important task. While many have mentioned simple institutional intransigence or even faculty hostility to legislative goals as reasons for slow progress, these are not sufficient to understand variation in this arena (Levine, 1997). The question at hand is this: Under what circumstances are institutions of higher education more or less likely to respond to state pressure to provide information on outcomes from the different forms of scholarship?

This chapter provides a framework to answer this question. The concepts and relationships that need to be defined will include the types of responses available to colleges and universities, the circumstances under which each response is more likely, and the particular context within higher education for both the pressures applied and the nature of each response.

This framework relies on Oliver's theory of strategic responses (1991). Oliver hypothesizes five strategic responses that can be undertaken by organizations in response to pressure applied from an institution. The specific pressure discussed in this chapter is external pressure from state policymakers for public colleges and universities to provide systematic evidence of outcomes.

Strategic Response: Theory

This framework uses Oliver's typology of strategic responses (1991) that organizations use when institutional pressures are enacted. Oliver hypothesized five strategic responses available to organizations: acquiescence, compromise, avoidance, defiance, and manipulation.

Types of Strategic Response. *Acquiescence* is the least active of the organizational responses to institutional pressures. Organizations may acquiesce out of habit, through imitation, or through compliance. Imitation and compliance may not involve much active thought or planning; compliance is a more active form of acquiescence.

Organizations may also choose to *compromise* with institutional pressures. The tactics used in compromising are balancing, pacifying, and bargaining. Balancing seeks to achieve parity among multiple stakeholders. Pacifying typically involves minor levels of resistance to pressure while attempting to placate institutional pressures. The most active form of compromise is bargaining.

When an organization uses *avoidance* as a response to institutional pressures, it attempts to "preclude the necessity of conformity" (Oliver, 1991, p. 154). The tactics available to fulfill this response are concealment, buffering, and escape. Concealment involves creating the appearance rather than the fact of conformity. Buffering consists of an attempt to isolate the technical activities of the organization from external contact. The last form of avoidance available to organizations is escape, in which "an organization may exit the domain in which pressure is exerted" (Oliver, 1991, p. 155).

Moving along the scale of organizational response to institutional pressure, the next, and more active, form of response is *defiance*. An organization may choose to defy pressure by dismissal, challenge, or attack. In dismissing pressure, an organization would decide that the penalties for noncompliance are low and that an organizational challenge allows the organization to "make a virtue of [its] insurrection" (Oliver, 1991, p. 156). Organizations using challenge as a tactic may define themselves by their refusal to conform to pressures. Attack is distinguished by the "intensity and aggressiveness of the organization's active departure from institutional pressures and expectations" (Oliver, 1991, p. 157).

The last strategic response to institutional pressure in Oliver's typology is *manipulation*. An organization that attempts to manipulate institutional pressures seeks to "change or exert power over the content of the expectations themselves" (Oliver, 1991, p. 157). One tactic available to manipulate expectations is co-optation. This tactic involves changing the institution that is creating pressure to align it with the organization's interests. Another tactic used in this type of response is influence, which includes changing the definitions or criteria for performance. The last tactic available to organizations that choose to use a manipulative response is control—the use of forceful measures to realign the institution that creates pressure.

Predictors of Strategic Response. In addition to her typology of strategic responses, Oliver (1991) hypothesizes a set of antecedents of strategic response. She posits that each aspect of institutional pressure will condition the type of response that can be expected from organizations. Oliver's five antecedents are cause, constituents, content, control, and context (Table 7.1).

Institutional pressures typically have one of two objectives: social acceptability or economic accountability and rationalization. An organization will be more likely to choose strategic responses other than acquiescence when the anticipated increase in social legitimacy or economic efficiency is low.

With regard to constituents, Oliver hypothesizes two separate possible relationships between institutional pressures and organizational response. If an organization faces pressures from a variety of sources, the possibility of acquiescing becomes low. A second relationship that occurs with regard to institutional constituency has to do with resource dependence: substantial dependence on the pressuring institutions for resources will result in acquiescence.

Another important predictive factor in looking at organizational response is the content of the pressure. A pressure that is in line with the self-perceptions and stated objectives of an organization is much more likely to be palatable. Related to this, if an institutional pressure causes a decline

Table 7.1. Summary of Oliver's Strategic Responses to Institutional Pressures

Institutional Factor	Research Question	Predictive Dimensions	Strategic Response
Cause	Why is the organization being pressured to conform to institutional rules or expectations?	Legitimacy or social fitness Efficiency or economic fitness	*Legitimacy:* Low legitimacy = high resistance *Efficiency:* Small efficiency gains = high resistance
Constituents	Who is exerting institutional pressures on the organization?	Multiplicity of constituent demands Dependence on institutional constituents	*Multiplicity:* Single or few constituents = low resistance *Dependency:* High levels of dependency = low resistance
Content	To what norms or requirements is the organization being pressured to conform?	Consistency with organizational goals Discretionary constraints imposed on the organization	*Consistency:* Very consistent = low resistance *Constraints:* Few constraints = low resistance
Control	How or by what means are the institutional pressures being exerted?	Legal coercion or enforcement Voluntary diffusion of norms	*Coercion:* High coercion = low resistance *Diffusion:* Strong norms = low resistance
Context	What is the environmental context within which institutional pressures are being exerted?	Environmental uncertainty Environmental interconnectedness	*Uncertainty:* High uncertainty = low resistance *Interconnectedness:* Highly interconnected = low resistance

Source: Oliver (1991).

in an organization's ability to perform its core operations with some discretion, the organization will be more likely to resist.

The degree to which a pressure can be brought to bear on an organization also plays a role in whether it will be met with resistance. Legal coercion is one way to bring pressure. Similarly, the degree to which an institutional norm is voluntarily adopted by organizational actors will play a role in the degree of resistance that organizations offer.

Oliver's last two hypotheses have to do with the environmental context in which both the institution and the organization operate. Uncertainty in the environment, which leads to an inability to predict events accurately, will also increase the likelihood of institutional resistance. An environment that has low levels of interconnectedness will lead to higher levels of organizational resistance.

Oliver's typology and her hypotheses about the possible relationships between factors in institutional pressures and organizational response form the structure for the framework developed in this chapter. The next step is to connect this theory to the literature on state policy and its possible effects on the institutionalization of Boyer's domains of scholarship, with particular emphasis on the scholarships of teaching, discovery, and application.

The Domain of Teaching: Strategic Responses to Assessment

To understand the processes behind colleges' and universities' accepting or resisting state pressures to assess student outcomes, Oliver's typology will be used to analyze the types of strategies that institutions of higher education might use to acquiesce to or resist such an institutional pressure and to understand under what circumstances such an acceptance or resistance might be more or less likely. The literature on assessment for accountability in higher education will be used to provide illustrations or counterexamples for the hypothesized relationships that Oliver set out.

Causes as Predictive Factors. Oliver's first hypothesis states that there is a direct relationship between the degree of social legitimacy to be gained from conformity and the level of acquiescence on the part of organizations. For higher education to acquiesce to a state-mandated external assessment of student outcomes, organizations must perceive that social legitimacy, in the form of public confidence and approval, will follow. Although authors have tied increasing public criticism of higher education to the need for external accountability for student outcomes, the literature is far from clear on the ways in which this type of accountability would contribute to the already high social legitimacy of institutions of higher education (Graham, Lyman, and Trow, 1995; Nettles, 1995).

Oliver hypothesizes that a perceived increase in organizational efficiency would also increase the likelihood of acquiescence. Much of the literature on external assessment of student outcomes for the purposes of accountability suggests that the primary reason to undertake such an assessment would be to demonstrate to the state the productivity of the institution (Guthrie, 1990).

The pressure from the state to provide this type of outcome information would seem to be more useful for the state in determining the efficiency of colleges and universities rather than improving the efficiency of these institutions. It seems likely that the perceived increase in efficiency for colleges and universities in acquiescing to this type of pressure would be low and would thus reduce the likelihood of compliance.

Constituents as Predictive Factors. A negative relationship is expected between the number of constituents involved and the level of acquiescence on the part of organizations. Higher education as an enterprise faces multiple constituents: demands from state government, professional organizations, accreditors, students, and the federal government all play a role in the decision making of colleges and universities. Responding to state pressure for assessment of student outcomes may conflict with demands from professional organizations to respect the autonomy of faculty members. Oliver (1991) suggests that avoidance, and concealment in particular, may be one of the preferred strategic responses in this type of situation, as it allows the organization to give the appearance of acquiescence to multiple demands without changing any core operations.

Resource dependence is hypothesized to be one of the key predictive factors in organizational acquiescence to outside pressures. A review of the literature on higher education assessment suggests that the ability of the state to provide funding based on colleges' and universities' compliance with pressure to provide student outcomes funding is a key predictor of acquiescence. The example of South Carolina is illustrative in this regard. At one time, public institutions in the state were funded based on their performance on thirty-seven performance indicators (Ewell and Riis, 2000). The ability of the state in this case to tie compliance to funding, and the dependence of institutions on the state for funding, made it likely that institutions would comply. States that make an explicit link between funding for institutions and the existence of student outcomes measures may be more likely to have acquiescent institutions.

Contents as Predictive Factors. The content of pressure is critical in the level of compliance to be expected. In the case of assessing student outcomes, the content of the pressure will most likely be at odds with the core values of the academy. This reason, more than any other, has been mentioned in the literature on assessment of student outcomes as an important feature of higher education's resistance to state pressure for student outcomes information. Boud (1990) discusses the disjuncture between assessment practices and academic values. Boud states that in academic practice, there are several closely held principles that rarely make their way into the practice of assessment: critical evaluation of ideas, peer judgment, an emphasis on process rather than outcome, and personal responsibility for the authenticity of work. Because assessment practices are so markedly different from the professional life of academic workers, it becomes less and less likely that pressure for increased assessment will be met with compliance.

Many outcome assessments are divorced from the disciplinary base out of which most academics operate. Faculty members can be said to have at least divided allegiance between their discipline and their institution (Clark, 1993). Because the content of most existing student outcome assessment processes is at cross purposes with many academic values, pressure to implement such an assessment would most likely lead to increased levels of resistance, with organizations tending toward strategic responses like manipulation or defiance rather than sacrificing core values such as academic practice or disciplinary focus.

The content of student outcome assessment may also be problematic for organizations of higher education in that it conflicts with core operations in these organizations. Ewell (1999) discusses the difficulty of implementing an assessment program in the state of New Jersey: "I recall one faculty member at a state college in New Jersey characterizing the state's position, and his own reaction, succinctly: 'this [assessment program] is so wonderful that we're going to *make* you do it!'" (p.149).

Faculty perceive that they should be the primary assessors and evaluators of student outcomes and that external evaluators may be perceived as infringing on this core process of the organization (Honan and Teferra, 2001). To the extent that external assessment measures are perceived as infringing on the core activity of teaching and learning, Oliver's framework would suggest that faculty will resist their implementation.

Control as a Predictive Factor. The degree to which a state can exercise control over institutions of higher education varies tremendously by state (McGuiness, Epper, and Arredondo, 1994). A positive relationship between the ability to use legal coercion and levels of compliance is hypothesized in Oliver's work. States where institutions have high levels of autonomy, particularly in the form of constitutional autonomy, can expect less compliance with pressures of any kind (Richardson, Bracco, Callan, and Finney, 1999).

States have typically had varying success in exerting control over behavior at institutions of higher education through the voluntary diffusion of norms and values. However, there are some counterexamples to this trend. Missouri's emphasis on student assessment seems to have been adopted voluntarily by Truman State University, a campus that is preoccupied with the measurement of student outcomes (Trombley, 2001). More research is needed on the mechanisms used to diffuse the norms from the state in the higher education environment before any definitive conclusions can be drawn.

Environment as a Predictive Factor. The last relationships that Oliver hypothesized between pressures and levels of compliance have to do with the environmental context in which pressure is being placed. The first environmental context is uncertainty: in an uncertain environment, organizations are likely to acquiesce. Probably the key uncertainty facing colleges and universities is financing (Honan and Teferra, 2001; Burke, 1998; Guthrie, 1990). Institutions of higher education are dependent on the state for resources and facing an uncertain environment in terms of the financing of higher education. Both the nature of the constituents and the nature of the environment may lead toward organizational acquiescence in this situation.

Another factor in the environmental context related to organizational compliance is the degree of interconnectedness among organizations. Oliver hypothesizes that a high level of interconnectedness will be associated with high levels of compliance.

The hypothesis that systems with high levels of connections will be more likely to acquiesce would seem to be operative in higher education: Richardson, Bracco, Callan, and Finney (1999) found that more unified systems were more likely to respond to state priorities.

At this point, it seems likely that most of the push for institutional accountability in the realm of student learning will come from external groups, with an emphasis on determining the efficiency of higher education and a focus on broad, nondisciplinary learning outcomes. I hypothesize that the most likely response from colleges and universities will be resistance, probably in the form of concealment. Colleges and universities will put on an outward show of compliance, with little actual change to organizational processes. The only possible exception would be if there is a large amount of resource dependence coupled with accountability for those resources. In that case, it seems more than likely to me that colleges and universities will be more likely to acquiesce to these pressures.

The Domain of Discovery: Strategic Responses to Demands for Research Productivity

Another key area for policymakers in many states is research productivity (Dundar and Lewis, 1998). State policymakers, much as in the area of assessment of student learning, want to know that they are receiving a good return on their investment in higher education (Ludwig, 1996). The ongoing difficulties in funding higher education will make it more likely that state policymakers will step in to attempt to hold colleges and universities accountable for their research output.

At one level, this could be seen as an unwarranted and unwelcome intrusion of the state into a province that is one of the key areas for the autonomy of institutions of higher education. Few values are more cherished than *lehrfreiheit*, the ability of researchers to investigate areas of their choosing, in the manner in which they choose, subject only to the review of their peers (Kerr, 2001).

Yet this area too could be one in which the state plays a positive role, helping colleges and universities to institutionalize this domain of scholarship. One of the key outcomes that state policymakers may be able to aid would be the institutionalization of the scholarship of discovery in colleges where the primary emphasis has been teaching. Changing state priorities may make it possible for faculty in these institutions to have changing reward structures that emphasize the domain of discovery as one of their key responsibilities (Clark and Rockefeller Foundation, 1987).

Causes as Predictive Factors. As Oliver (1991) suggests, there are two predictive dimensions when considering causes as predictive factors: legitimacy and efficiency. The first is the perceived legitimacy of the institutional pressure. In this case, how will faculty view state demands for increasing research productivity at all institutions in the state? While few faculty at research institutions would view the goal of increased research productivity with skepticism, many might object to the state's role in emphasizing this goal (Alexander, 2000; Banta, Rudolph, Van Dyke, and Fisher, 1996). At other types of institutions, however, faculty are typically more likely to view the state as a legitimate actor in setting goals for faculty activity (Layzell, 1996). Thus, the legitimacy of state demands in this area will depend critically on the type of college or university where faculty are employed.

The second predictive dimension is efficiency. In the scholarship of discovery, is it likely that college leaders and faculty will perceive that there are economic benefits to be realized from an increased emphasis on the scholarship of discovery? Certainly research institutions have proven themselves to be quite entrepreneurial in seeking out external funding for the support of the scholarship of discovery (Kerr, 2001; Slaughter and Leslie, 1997; Slaughter and Rhoades, 2004). Other types of colleges and universities would most likely therefore perceive genuine economic benefits to be realized by conforming to state demands for increasing productivity in the area of the scholarship of discovery.

Constituents as Predictive Factors. Oliver (1991) contends that the nature of an organization's constituency will determine in large part the degree to which the organization will acquiesce to or resist an institutional demand for change. In the case of state demands for research productivity, much of the institutional response will depend on the degree to which colleges and universities see their constituents as other members of the academic community or whether they identify their constituents as primarily being their patrons in state government.

Research institutions almost certainly see themselves as having multiple constituents, including the state, students, other research institutions, and faculty. Since their responsibilities extend across all of these multiple constituents, it seems unlikely that faculty or college leaders would readily acquiesce to the demands of any single constituency (Metzger, 1987). Nevertheless, community colleges and comprehensive institutions may indeed view the state as their primary constituent; this most likely depends on the degree to which the institution is supported by state revenues: colleges and universities that are primarily resource dependent on the state will be far more likely to view state policymakers as their primary constituents (Pfeffer and Salancik, 1978).

Content as a Predictive Factor. The content of the institutional demands on organizations is thought to be key in determining organizational response. To the degree that the content of the challenge is consistent with organizational goals, there will be substantial acquiescence. Also, the level of constraint imposed by virtue of the institutional demands will be a critical determinant of organizational response.

As state policymakers think about implementing accountability for research productivity, it is worth remembering that the content of this challenge will be critical to its success (Presley and Engelbride, 1998). Academics are most likely quite receptive to the overall goal of research productivity, and therefore measures to encourage this behavior are quite consistent with organizational goals.

However, academics are hostile to the notion of directed activity in the scholarship of discovery. State policy activities that held organizations accountable for the type of research completed or the outlets for that research will almost certainly be met with fierce resistance from academic organizations, as these kinds of constraints are anathema to the concept of academic freedom (Rhoades, 2001).

Control as a Predictive Factor. Oliver (1991) posits two distinct methods of institutional control over organizational processes. The first is legal control, whereby organizational behavior can be controlled by direct government mandate. The second is the voluntary diffusion of institutional norms or practices.

In the context of encouraging research productivity, there are certainly some possibilities for state policymakers to engage in legalistic mandating of behaviors. For instance, states could mandate a certain amount of research as measured by journal articles or number of patents (Rhoades, 2001; Webster and Conrad, 1986). However, historical precedent and current experience suggest that the actual degree of legalistic control over organizations of higher education is relatively low. Very few states have the means or opportunity to mandate a process as complex as research productivity (Presley and Engelbride, 1998; Richardson, Bracco, Callan, and Finney, 1999).

Nevertheless, it may be possible for states to diffuse institutional norms of behavior, for instance, by establishing and promoting best practices with regard to research productivity. This practice would encourage an overall push for institutional isomorphism (Dey, Milem, and Berger, 1997). Other studies have shown that established state policy environments do affect institutional-level behaviors, suggesting that one of the most promising ways to institutionalize the scholarship of discovery would be the promulgation of norms of behavior, as opposed to strict mandates for certain behaviors (Burke, 2002).

Context as Predictive Factors. The last domain of predictive factors to consider when thinking about state policymaking to encourage the scholarship of discovery is the context in which these institutional pressures are placed on individual organizations.

The context for higher education institutions is beset by continued uncertainty. This applies equally to the scholarship of discovery, where research funding is uncertain and priorities among alternative funders may shift unpredictably (Slaughter and Leslie, 1997). The uncertain environment in which institutions of higher education find themselves will continue to encourage acquiescence in this area (Presley and Engelbride, 1998). As with the area of student assessment, the degree of interconnectedness should also affect acquiescence to state demands. States where institutions share a common governance framework therefore ought to be able to enhance research productivity more effectively than their counterparts without such a framework (Layzell, 1996; McGuiness, Epper, and Arredondo, 1994; Richardson, Bracco, Callan, and Finney, 1999).

It seems to me that most institutions will be likely to acquiesce to many of the demands that could be placed on them for increased research productivity, provided that these demands are not for specific types of research but rather in encouraging more and better research overall for institutions. To the extent that they engage in research, comprehensive institutions would be the most likely to acquiesce to these demands, since states are one of the few large stakeholders in these institutions.

Research institutions, reflecting their broader constituent base, are more likely to attempt some form of compromise with state policymakers. This could include activities like a performance funding program that rewards institutions that receive the most grant dollars. This type of compromise would provide incentives for research institutions to engage in activities that already enjoy high levels of legitimacy among faculty, while at the same time giving state policymakers a hand in leveraging the research productivity of institutions.

The Domain of Application: Strategic Responses to State Demands for Industry Collaboration

Industry collaboration is another area of high priority for state policymakers at this point in time. Many state policymakers view ongoing collaboration between industries and colleges and universities as promising means of economic development (Etzkowitz, Webster, and Healey, 1998). This section reviews the five antecedents of strategic response that Oliver (1991) proposed and the implications of each for the institutionalization of this particular instance of the scholarship of application.

Causes as Predictive Factors. As with the other two areas of scholarship, the causes of institutional pressure for industry collaboration will play a large role in the strategic responses of colleges and universities. Again, legitimacy and efficiency of the cause play a key role here.

Institutions of higher education are likely to see the causes of pressure for industry collaboration as legitimate to the extent that they coincide with core academic values. Industry collaboration that is seen primarily as a means of generating additional revenue through licensing fees or contract work is not likely to be supported by academics (Etzkowitz, Webster, and Healey, 1998). However, industry collaboration that is seen as a legitimate scholarly activity, particularly one in the domain of the scholarship of application, is likely to be supported (Elliott, 1995).

As with legitimacy, the perceived efficiency of a given pressure on organizations is thought to be key by Oliver. For many inside higher education, industry collaboration is among the most lucrative possible activities (Etzkowitz, Webster, and Healey, 1998; Slaughter and Leslie, 1997; Slaughter and Rhoades, 2004). Little resistance ought to be encountered to the idea that expanding the scholarship of application in this way is worthwhile. Most resistance in the area of cause will come about because of concerns about the legitimacy of institutional pressure for industry collaboration.

Constituents as Predictive Factors. Local businesses or related industries are not often thought of as constituents of colleges and universities. (For an interesting exception to this postulate in the area of life sciences and biotechnology, see Owen-Smith, Riccaboni, Pammoli, and Powell, 2002.) To the extent that colleges are serving multiple constituencies, few of which are among the possible industry partners, the more likely it is that state policymakers will encounter resistance to pressure for increased collaboration.

Content as a Predictive Factor. Most industry-college collaborations occur around a multidisciplinary framework. For instance, a collaboration with a computer parts maker may involve professors from departments of management, engineering, and computer science. This format could constitute a strength or a weakness of content as a predictive factor (Riis, 2001).

Multidisciplinarity, if used to equally value the different domains of academic expertise, could enhance the likelihood of acquiescence on the part of colleges and universities. However, if a multidisciplinary approach means that the form of the scholarship of application will be devoid of disciplinary content, this could lead to high levels of resistance to institutional pressures.

Control as a Predictive Factor. When discussing control, Oliver (1991) suggests that two types will be critical in determining the strategic response of organizations: coercive and diffusion based. Coercive measures would seem to be particularly unsuited to the practice of industry collaboration and, by extension, the scholarship of application. Given the widely varying circumstances of colleges and universities and the tacit structure of most collaborations, mandatory reforms in this area seem unlikely. However, diffusion of this practice through shared norms and values would seem to be a particularly valuable approach (Owen-Smith, Riccaboni, Pammoli, and Powell, 2002).

If state policymakers can signal through a variety of means that industry collaboration is a valued and worthwhile activity for colleges and universities, it seems likely that more organizational leaders will engage in these practices. Such practices could help to further institutionalize the scholarship of application.

Context as a Predictive Factor.   Continued uncertainty in the environment for institutions of higher education will almost certainly encourage them to pick up the noted norms of collaboration if they are extensively promoted by state policymakers. Colleges and universities need to seek tighter connections with the outside world in order to establish their own security, both financial and political, but they do so at great cost to their own internal dynamics (Kerr, 2001).

The interconnectedness of systems of higher education should play a role as state policymakers seek to extend the scholarship of application through industry collaboration. More tightly connected systems should be more responsive in this area, as they are predicted to be responsive in the other areas under consideration in this chapter.

It seems most likely that colleges and universities will be responsive to calls for more collaboration with industry to the extent that these pressures are tied to core academic values. If industry collaboration is simply a lucrative add-on that will supplement funding from other sources, its legitimacy for academics will be quite limited, and resistance is likely to be high. However, if institutional pressure for more university-industry collaboration takes the form of sharing of best practices and is tied to the more traditional understanding of Boyer's scholarship of application, colleges and university leaders will be far more likely to acquiesce.

Conclusion

Can state policymakers aid in the process of institutionalizing Boyer's view of scholarship? The analysis in this chapter suggests that this is a strong possibility, but only if policymakers are sensitive to the types of predictive factors that may create differing strategic responses from institutions. Table 7.2 summarizes the predictive factors at play in each of the three domains of scholarship and likely strategic responses from colleges and universities depending on the type and form of policies put into place.

Institutional research is likely to play a large role in any call for increased accountability from state policymakers. Institutional researchers

Table 7.2. Summary of Higher Education's Expected Response to State Policies for Changing Scholarship

	Scholarship of Teaching: Student Assessment	Scholarship of Discovery: Emphasis on Research Productivity	Scholarship of Application: Encouraging Collaboration with Industry
Cause	*Legitimacy:* Probably low *Efficiency:* Expected to be low	*Legitimacy:* Depends on type of college or university *Efficiency:* Probably high	*Legitimacy:* As long as they are consistent with core academic values *Efficiency:* Highly efficient; low resistance on this dimension
Constituents	*Multiplicity:* Multiple constituents mean lower acquiescence *Dependence:* Contingent on states' linking funding to compliance	*Multiplicity:* For research institutions, multiple constituents mean less compliance *Dependence:* For community colleges and comprehensives, dependence means compliance	*Multiplicity:* Depends on connections to and relationship with local industry *Dependence:* Organizational type is key
Content	*Consistency:* Low consistency ensures resistance *Constraint:* Many possible constraints; also increasing resistance	*Consistency:* Fairly consistent with organizational goals *Constraint:* Specific direction (for example, hours in office) will be met with resistance	*Consistency:* Support for multidiscipline activity must be signaled *Constraint:* No likely constraints
Control	*Coercion:* Low compliance without strong state governance *Diffusion:* Mixed; depends on organization type	*Coercion:* Legalistic control will mean higher resistance *Diffusion:* Shared norms and values could result in lower resistance	*Coercion:* Mandatory collaboration not possible *Diffusion:* Could be quite promising
Context	*Uncertainty:* Continued uncertainty ensures some level of compliance *Interconnectedness:* Nature of higher education governance system is key	*Uncertainty:* High levels of uncertainty, meaning compliance is more likely *Interconnectedness:* Governance framework critical	*Uncertainty:* Uncertainty helps with compliance *Interconnectedness:* To the extent that a framework for diffusion is available, diffusion is effective

Sources: Oliver (1991); this chapter.

are uniquely placed to provide the information on which decisions about compliance or avoidance of state policymakers' mandates will be made.

However, institutional researchers will not play a passive role in these activities. Rather, they will be in a position to shape both the nature of policymakers' demands for accountability and the form of the response that colleges and universities will display. They will most likely need to be creative interpreters of both institutional demands for increased accountability and the strategic responses of colleges and universities. In this role, they may be able to manage the flow of information between these two groups in a way that creates mutual benefits.

Boyer (1999) discusses the roles of college presidents, accrediting agencies, and professional associations in reshaping the academic field in order to encourage the development of all four domains of scholarship. But he cautions that only faculty are in a position to truly reshape their own profession. Nevertheless, although faculty must have the final decision regarding any redefinition of the academic profession, there is a role for state policy to play in encouraging the institutionalization of the different domains of scholarship.

Overall, state policy may be a promising area to encourage further development of the domains of scholarship within colleges and universities. In each of the areas I describe, I believe that there are useful roles for state policy to play in setting the basic framework within which organizational actors may be able to change the way different forms of scholarship are understood and rewarded.

References

Alexander, F. K. "The Changing Face of Accountability." *Journal of Higher Education,* 2000, 71(4), 411–431.

Banta, T. W., Rudolph, L. B., Van Dyke, J., and Fisher, H. S. "Performance Funding Comes of Age in Tennessee." *Journal of Higher Education,* 1996, 67(1), 23–45.

Boud, D. "Assessment and the Promotion of Academic Values." *Studies in Higher Education,* 1990, 15(1), 101–111.

Boyer, E. L. *Scholarship Reconsidered: Priorities of the Professoriate.* Princeton, N.J.: Carnegie Foundation for the Advancement of Teaching, 1990.

Burke, J. C. "Performance Funding Indicators: Concerns, Values and Models for State Colleges and Universities." In J. C. Burke and A. Serban (eds.), *Performance Funding for Public Higher Education.* New Directions for Institutional Research, no. 97. San Francisco: Jossey-Bass, 1998.

Burke, J. C. *Funding Public Colleges and Universities for Performance.* Albany, N.Y.: Rockefeller Institute Press, 2002.

Clark, B. "The Problem of Complexity in Modern Higher Education." In S. Rothblatt and B. Wittrock (eds.), *The European and American University Since 1800: Historical and Sociological Essays.* Cambridge: Cambridge University Press, 1993.

Clark, B. R., and Rockefeller Foundation. *The Academic Profession: National, Disciplinary, and Institutional Settings.* Berkeley: University of California Press, 1987.

Dey, E. L., Milem, J. F., and Berger, J. B. "Changing Patterns of Publication Productivity: Accumulative Advantage or Institutional Isomorphism?" *Sociology of Education,* 1997, *70*(4), 308–323.

Dundar, H., and Lewis, D. R. "Determinants of Research Productivity in Higher Education." *Research in Higher Education,* 1998, *39*(6), 607–631.

Elliott, C. "Exploitation or Partnership? An Alternative Approach to University-Industry Collaboration." *Industry and Higher Education,* 1995, *9*(1), 39–41.

Etzkowitz, H., Webster, A., and Healey, P. *Capitalizing Knowledge: New Intersections of Industry and Academia.* Albany, N.Y.: State University of New York Press, 1998.

Ewell, P. "Assessment of Higher Education Quality: Promise and Politics." In S. Messick (ed.), *Assessment in Higher Education.* Mahwah, N.J.: Erlbaum, 1999.

Ewell, P., and Riis, P. *Assessing Student Learning Outcomes: A Supplement to Measuring Up 2000.* San Jose: National Center for Public Policy and Higher Education, 2000.

Graham, P. A., Lyman, R. W., and Trow, M. *Accountability of Colleges and Universities.* New York: Columbia University, 1995.

Guthrie, J. W. "The Evolving Political Economy of Education and the Implications for Educational Evaluation." *Educational Review,* 1990, *42*(2), 109–131.

Honan, J. P., and Teferra, D. "The US Academic Profession: Key Policy Changes." *Higher Education,* 2001, *41,* 183–203.

Kerr, C. *The Uses of the University.* (5th ed.) Cambridge, Mass.: Harvard University Press, 2001.

Layzell, D. T. "Faculty Workload and Productivity: Recurrent Issues with New Imperatives." *Review of Higher Education,* 1996, *19*(3), 267–281.

Levine, A. (1997, Jan. 31) "Higher Education's New Status as a Mature Industry." *Chronicle of Higher Education,* p. A48.

Ludwig, M. J. (1996). "Framing the Public Policy Debate on Faculty: What Is the Role of Research?" in J. M. Braxton (ed.), *Faculty Teaching and Research: Is There a Conflict?* New Directions for Institutional Research, no. 90. San Francisco: Jossey-Bass, 1996.

McGuiness, A. C., Epper, R. M., and Arredondo, S. *State Postsecondary Education Structures Handbook.* Denver: Education Commission of the States, 1994.

Metzger, W. P. "The Academic Profession in the United States." In B. R. Clark (ed.), *The Academic Profession.* Berkeley: University of California Press, 1987.

Nettles, M. T. "The Emerging National Policy Agenda on Higher Education Assessment: A Wake Up Call." *Review of Higher Education,* 1995, *18*(3), 293–313.

Oliver, C. "Strategic Reponses to Institutional Processes." *Journal of Management Review,* 1991, *16*(1), 145–179.

Owen-Smith, J., Riccaboni, M., Pammoli, F., and Powell, W. W. "A Comparison of U.S. and European University-Industry Relations in the Life Sciences." *Management Science,* 2002, *48*(1), 24–43.

Pfeffer, J., and Salancik, G. R. *The External Control of Organizations: A Resource Dependence Perspective.* New York: HarperCollins, 1978.

Presley, J. B., and Engelbride, E. "Accounting for Faculty Productivity in the Research University." *Review of Higher Education,* 1998, *22*(1), 17–37.

Rhoades, G. "Managing Productivity in an Academic Institution: Rethinking the Whom, Which, What, and Whose of Productivity." *Research in Higher Education,* 2001, *42*(5), 619–632.

Richardson, R., Bracco, K. R., Callan, P., and Finney, J. (1999). *Designing State Higher Education Systems for a New Century.* Phoenix, Ariz.: American Council on Education/Oryx Press.

Riis, J. O. "Stimulating Manufacturing Excellence Through University-Industry Interaction: Problem-Based Learning at Aalborg University, Denmark." *Industry and Higher Education,* 2001, *15*(6), 385–392.

Slaughter, S., and Leslie, L. L. *Academic Capitalism: Politics, Policies, and the Entrepreneurial University.* Baltimore, Md.: Johns Hopkins University Press, 1997.

Slaughter, S., and Rhoades, G. *Academic Capitalism and the New Economy: Markets, State, and Higher Education.* Baltimore, Md.: Johns Hopkins University Press, 2004.

Trombley, W. "Trying to Measure Student Learning." *National Crosstalk,* Summer 2001, p. 1.

Webster, D. S., and Conrad, C. F. "Using Faculty Research Performance for Academic Quality Rankings." In J. W. Cresswell (ed.), *Measuring Faculty Research Performance.* New Directions for Institutional Research, no. 50. San Francisco: Jossey-Bass, 1986.

WILLIAM R. DOYLE is assistant professor of higher education in the Department of Leadership, Policy and Organizations, Peabody College of Vanderbilt University.

INDEX

Abbott, R. D., 54
Accountability, 101, 102
Acquiescence: and context of pressures, 107; definition of, 98; and social legitimacy, 101
Adaptation function, 25–26
Administrators: and challenges of scholarship of teaching, 40–41; and changes in rewards, 79; and faculty productivity evaluations, 31; goal of, 91; importance of, 80; and importance of application, 48; power of, 46; survey of, 80–81
Alexander, F. K., 105
American Association of Higher Education, 39
American Indian Housing Initiative (AIHI), 13–14
Anderson, M. S., 55
Application, scholarship of: challenges of, 41; definition of, 1; ethics in, 57; focus on, in doctoral education, 54–55; and fragmentation of work, 9; importance of, 9, 47–48; overview of, 52; strategic responses regarding, 107–109; and value patterns, 70–76
Arnold, G. B., 90
Arredondo, S., 103, 107
Assessment. See Evaluation; Evaluation, of domains
Assistant professors, 9
Atkinson, M. P., 48
Attacking, 99
Attitudes, 43–45
Audits, 75
Austin, A. E., 4, 51, 54, 55, 60
Avoidance, 98

Badley, G., 39, 48
Balancing, 98
Banta, T. W., 105
Bargaining, 98
Barton, R., 14
Bauer, T., 92
Benjamin, J., 43, 48
Bensimon, E. M., 79
Berberet, J., 78, 91

Berger, J. B., 106
Bergquist, W. H., 79
Biggs, B. A., 12
Birnbaum, R., 79, 85, 93
Blackburn, R. T., 79
Bloomgarden, A., 93
Bolman, L. G., 79, 85
Boud, D., 102
Boyer, E. L., 1–2, 4, 5, 8, 10, 16, 21, 51, 52, 58, 67, 68, 74, 77–78, 79, 80, 83, 88, 91, 97, 111
Bracco, K. R., 103, 106, 107
Brailow, D., 78, 91
Braskamp, L., 78, 91
Braxton, J. M., 1, 2, 3–4, 5, 9, 22, 23, 24, 28, 38, 44, 52, 53, 55, 56, 67, 68, 74, 78, 79, 80
Buffering, 98–99
Burke, J. C., 107

Calder, L., 25
Callan, P., 103, 106, 107
Cambridge, B., 29, 39, 48
Carnegie Academy for the Scholarship of Teaching and Learning (CASTL), 25, 39, 43
Carnegie Foundation for the Advancement of Teaching, 39, 63
Carnegie Scholar Program, 41
Center for the Integration of Research, Teaching, and Learning (CIRTL), 60–61
Centra, J., 28
Certificates, 61, 63
Challenging, 99
Checkoway, B., 9
Chemistry education, 9–10
Chief Dull Knife College, 13–14
CIRTL. See Center for the Integration of Research, Teaching, and Learning (CIRTL)
Civic engagement, 14
Clark, B. R., 79, 80, 81, 83, 103
Clark, S. E., 23, 25, 26
Cognitive psychologists, 25
Cohen, J., 8, 11, 12, 15, 17
Colbeck, C. L., 2–3, 7, 9, 10, 12, 14, 16

Back Issue/Subscription Order Form

Copy or detach and send to:

Jossey-Bass, A Wiley Imprint, 989 Market Street, San Francisco CA 94103-1741
Call or fax toll-free: Phone 888-378-2537 6:30AM–3PM PST; Fax 888-481-2665

Back Issues: Please send me the following issues at $29 each
(Important: please include ISBN number for each issue.)

_____

_____

_____

$ _____ Total for single issues

$ _____ SHIPPING CHARGES: SURFACE   Domestic   Canadian
                                First Item $5.00 $6.00
                                Each Add'l Item $3.00 $1.50

For next-day and second-day delivery rates, call the number listed above.

Subscriptions   Please ___ start ___ renew my subscription to *New Directions*
                  for Institutional Research for the year 2_____ at the following rate:

                  U.S.   ___ Individual $80   ___ Institutional $170
                  Canada   ___ Individual $80   ___ Institutional $210
                  All Others   ___ Individual $104   ___ Institutional $244

Online subscriptions are available via Wiley InterScience!

For more information about online subscriptions visit
www.interscience.wiley.com

$_____ Total single issues and subscriptions (Add appropriate sales tax for
your state for single issue orders. No sales tax for U.S. subscriptions.
Canadian residents, add GST for subscriptions and single issues.)

___ Payment enclosed (U.S. check or money order only)
___ VISA ___ MC ___ AmEx # _____ Exp. Date _____

Signature _____ Day Phone _____
___ Bill Me (U.S. institutional orders only. Purchase order required.)

Purchase order # _____

Federal Tax ID13559302   **GST 89102 8052**

Name _____

Address _____

_____

Phone _____ E-mail _____

For more information about Jossey-Bass, visit our Web site at www.josseybass.com